38135

38135

DEMCO

CULTURES OF THE WORLD

# PERU

*Kieran Falconer*

MARSHALL CAVENDISH

*New York • London • Sydney*

*38135*

Reference edition published 1999 by
Marshall Cavendish Corporation
99 White Plains Road
Tarrytown
New York 10591

© Times Editions Pte Ltd 1995

Originated and designed by
Times Books International, an imprint of
Times Editions Pte Ltd

Printed in Singapore

*Library of Congress Cataloging-in-Publication Data:*
Falconer, Kieran
    Peru / Kieran Falconer.
      p. cm.—(Cultures Of The World)
    Includes bibliographical references and index.
    Summary: Presents information on many aspects of this
South American country beginning with its geography and
history and including government, religion, arts, and food.
    ISBN 0-7614-0179-2 (lib. bdg.)
    1. Peru—Juvenile literature [1. Peru] I. Title.
II. Series.
F3408.5.F35   1995
985—dc20         95–14898
          CIP
          AC

# INTRODUCTION

THE REPUBLIC OF PERU is known as the center of perhaps the greatest ancient civilization of the Americas, the Incan empire. The glory of the Incas lives on in contemporary Peru—in its people, descendants of the Incas who carry on many of the traditions of their ancestors, in its artistic skills, and in the walls and buildings that still bear witness to the greatness of the Incas.

But Peru is not only a relic of past glories; it is also a modern country moving forward to take its place in the contemporary world. After a period of economic decline and social upheaval in the 1980s, Peru is today on its way to establishing political stability and economic independence. Peruvians have reason to look forward to the 21st century with the hope of seeing the reawakening of the Incan genius.

# CONTENTS

Schoolgirls in Lima.

# CONTENTS

**A Serrano woman spins wool on her front doorstep.**

# GEOGRAPHY

PERU IS THE THIRD LARGEST South American country, after Brazil and Argentina, and has the fourth largest population. It is a tropical country with its northern tip nearly touching the equator.

Peru has an area of about 496,222 square miles (1,285,215 square kilometers), nearly twice the size of Texas. Within its borders is found an astonishing range of geographic extremes: from one of the driest deserts in the world along the coast to the Amazon rainforest in the east. The Andes, which form the backbone of the country, are the world's second highest mountain range, and the Colca Canyon is twice as deep as the Grand Canyon. Lake Titicaca is the world's highest navigable lake.

This terrain presents formidable difficulties to its human inhabitants and especially to the farmers, who are at the mercy of a climate that varies from very hot to very cold. The terrain has also been a great obstacle in unifying the nation. People tend to remain isolated in their villages. Only recently have roads been built to link remote areas with the rest of the country.

*Opposite*: **Incan terraces line the Urubamba Valley. Like their ancestors, the present-day Andean people face a difficult life. Poor farming techniques, together with uncertain rainfall, low temperatures, and a stony soil, result in low yields of basic crops, such as corn, barley, quinoa, and potatoes.**

*Left*: **A desert landscape on the south coast. The Costa, or coastal region, receives less rain than the Sahara in north Africa, and there is very little agricultural activity.**

A large part of
Peru is covered by
mountains.
Because of the
high altitude, the
air is much
thinner, and
many new visitors
are affected by
soroche ("SAW-
roche"), or altitude
sickness, which
produces a feeling
of nausea.
The local people
have adapted to
the altitude over
generations by
developing thick
chests and large
lungs to efficiently
draw the limited
oxygen from the
air.

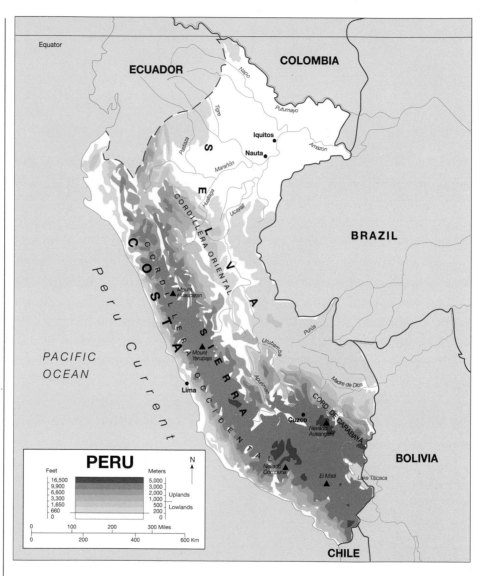

## GEOGRAPHIC REGIONS

Peru includes three main geographic areas: the Costa, a semiarid plain
along the Pacific Ocean; the Sierra, the mountainous Andes region; and
the Selva, the rainforest of the Amazon Basin to the east of the Andes.

The Costa is the thin fringe of land that lies between the Pacific Ocean
on the west and the Andes on the east. It varies in width from about 10
to 100 miles (16–160 kilometers) and covers just over 10% of the country.

It has become the most densely populated part of Peru, principally because Lima is located there. This small region has attracted nearly half the population of Peru because it offers a higher standard of living, employment opportunities, and a developed infrastructure.

Even though the Costa lies beside the ocean, the region is extremely dry and cool, with large stretches of arid plains. The main reason for this is the Peru Current, which brings cool water from the Antarctic, producing sea fogs but little rain. To the north is the Sechura Desert. Fishing is now one of the main occupations in the Costa. The immense schools of fish in the ocean compensate for the sterility of the Costa soil.

The Selva (meaning jungle) consists of the mountain slopes to the east of the Andes (the area is sometimes called the Montaña) and the Amazon Basin, which is primarily tropical rainforest. The Selva occupies nearly three-fifths of the country's territory yet is sparsely populated and little developed. The region is covered by lush vegetation and forest, which grows more profuse and dense as one journeys eastward. Hundreds of rivers and streams penetrate the jungle, and its inhabitants, native tribes, settle along the waterways. Rivers are the main highways because roads are quickly destroyed or overgrown. Navigation is hazardous and the water sometimes shallow, but the tribes rely on these rivers as a means to transport local produce, wood, and animals. The area is rich in timber, rubber, coffee, and tropical fruit. It is estimated that 80% of Peru's oil reserves are in this region, in addition to many mineral deposits.

**The Selva is hot and very humid but teems with wildlife and plants, which flourish probably because of the area's inaccessibility.**

Mt. Ausangate. The Andes are composed of towering ranges with snowcapped peaks, deep canyons with vertical sides, high, level plains, and active volcanoes in the south.

## THE ANDES: BACKBONE OF A CONTINENT

The Andes mountain chain is the longest continuous range in the world, extending more than 4,500 miles (7,240 kilometers) along the western side of South America and passing through many countries from the Isthmus of Panama in the north to Tierra del Fuego in the south. The Peruvian Central Andes, or Sierra, divides the dry coastal region from the tropical Amazon jungle in the east. The Sierra covers a quarter of Peru's surface. The highest mountains in this region are the snowcapped Huascarán at 22,205 feet (6,765 meters) and Yerupaja at 21,500 feet (6,550 meters), but the majority average around 12,000 feet (3,650 meters). The climate of the Sierra is as varied as the landscape. At higher altitudes, it can be freezing any month of the year, but it also gets hotter than the equator.

There are also many extinct and semiextinct volcanoes in the southern part of the highlands. These cone-shaped volcanoes continue southward along the western side of Lake Titicaca, and along the border with Chile and Bolivia. The snowtopped El Misti, at 18,000 feet (5,484 meters), is the third largest volcano in South America. It has not erupted for many years.

The word *andes* is thought to have come from the Incan word *andreres,* which refers to the terraces the Incas built on the sides of the mountains. This terraced system of agriculture enabled large areas of steep land to be cultivated. The system is still employed in some areas, and countless remains of ancient terracing give an insight into the productivity of this ancient civilization. Although at first sight they appear inhospitable to both people and farming, the Peruvian Andes paradoxically contain a variety of plant and animal life.

More people live in the Andes than in any other large highland region in the world. The highest habitation in the world is a shepherd's hut in the Andes at 17,000 feet (5,180 meters). Until recently, a majority of Peruvians lived in the Sierra. This has now decreased to one-third of the population.

The principal reason the Sierra is a population center is because the ancient Incan capital, Cuzco, was located high up in the Andes. Cuzco (meaning navel or center) is said to be the oldest city in South America. During the 13th to 16th centuries, when Incan civilization flourished, it was considered a sacred city and was the center of the Incan empire.

## *LAKES AND RIVERS*

Lake Titicaca has been a population center since before the Incas. At around 350 miles (560 kilometers) in length and 100 miles (160 kilometers) in width, Titicaca is so large it has waves like the sea. It contains more than 30 islands. Titicaca is Peru's main trade route with Bolivia. It lies at an elevation of 12,500 feet (3,810 meters), making it the world's highest navigable body of water.

Other natural trade routes include the many rivers that run through the Selva, some of them tributaries of the Amazon. The Marañón and Ucayali rivers begin 17,200 feet (5,240 meters) up in Peru's Andes, coming together near Nauta to form the Amazon, which then gradually plunges down waterfalls to the tropical rainforests that line most of the 2,200 miles (3,540 kilometers) it travels to the Atlantic Ocean.

**The rise in elevation on the Amazon is so gradual that small ships can reach the town of Iquitos from the Atlantic Ocean.**

## CITIES

Most of Peru's large cities are located in the coastal area. Lima, the capital, along with its port at Callao, contains over one-quarter of the population of Peru. Lima is also the commercial and educational center of Peru. Seventy percent of the nation's economic activity is located in Lima. It was founded in 1535 by the Spanish, who called it Ciudad de los Reyes, "City of Kings." Other large cities in the Costa include Trujillo, a commercial and industrial center, Chiclayo, and Chimbote.

Most of the cities of the Andes are small. The largest city is Arequipa, which has a major wool market. Cuzco is the ancient Incan capital located high in the Andes. It is the center of many Incan ruins.

The main town in the Selva is Iquitos, a river port on the Amazon. Although only 600 miles (965 kilometers) from Lima, Iquitos was so inaccessible before the advent of air travel that to get there from Lima required making a 7,000-mile (11,300-kilometer) journey through the Pacific to the Panama Canal, across the Caribbean, into the Atlantic, and finally up the Amazon.

Lima is laid out in the typical colonial pattern of streets leading to a central plaza. Its site was chosen on January 5, the eve of Epiphany, or the Feast of the Three Kings, hence its original name, "City of Kings."

*Below:* **A condor in flight and a three-toed sloth.**

*Opposite:* **A piranha shows its teeth.**

## *FLORA AND FAUNA*

Peru is teeming with wildlife. Southeast Peru has the greatest diversity of bird life of any place on the planet. The waters off the coast hold an abundant and diverse sea life, and along the coast vast numbers of seabirds come to feed on the ocean creatures.

Farther inland, the most famous Peruvian bird is the condor, a rare but beautiful sight in the Andes. It is a black bird with a white ruff and a wingspan of up to 10 feet (3 meters). As a member of the vulture family, the condor feeds on dead animals, but it will also sometimes kill its prey. It is not, however, a hunter and is unable to grasp or carry prey because its feet are similar to those of a chicken.

In the Andes, the equally famous llama was used for centuries as a pack animal before horses and donkeys were introduced. The Spanish brought many new animals to South America. Horses, cows, pigs, chickens, and cattle, none native to Peru, flourished when introduced. The Andes are also home to the puma or mountain lion. The puma was revered by the Incas as a symbol of power and elegance, but it has suffered more recently from indiscriminate hunting. Deer are also common, as is the Andean fox, which frequently raids both sheep herds and garbage cans.

The Selva has many different types of wildlife, including deer, jaguars, snakes, monkeys, colorful parrots, alligators, and flesh-eating piranhas. It has been little influenced by humans until recently. Its botanical diversity is such that it has an average of 500 different tree species per square mile. Tropical rainforests are the oldest continuous terrestrial habitat on earth, so plants have had much longer to evolve into different species. Although tropical rainforests presently cover less than 4% of the earth's surface, they are home to over 50% of all species.

## LLAMAS

Llamas are native to Peru and have been domesticated since prehistoric times, but it was the Incas who made the greatest use of them. They were used to carry burdens, as food, and for sacrifice in religious ceremonies; their wool and hide were used in clothing, and their dung for fuel.

Llamas are useful in the difficult Andean terrain because of their high tolerance for thirst, their endurance, and their ability to subsist on a wide variety of forage. However, when llamas are overloaded or exhausted, they will lie down, hiss, spit, and kick, refusing to move until they are relieved of some of the weight or until they are rested enough to continue the journey.

The llama's head resembles a camel's, with large eyes, a split nose, a harelip, and no upper teeth. Llamas range in color from the common pure white to black, with a range of mixtures of black, brown, and white in between. Their wool is still used for blankets and clothing.

But these animals and especially the Amazonian flora are all in danger of possible extinction by developers. Although tropical rainforests have been around for millions of years, within the last 100 years they have been on the decline. This is in direct relation to the growth in the human population. At the present rate of destruction, most of the remaining rainforests will be gone within the next 25 years. Although the rainforests look lush and healthy, they are extremely fragile, and if cleared for farmland, they rarely provide enough nutrients in the soil for more than five years of crops. Conservation has become a major concern. Peru now has about 5% of its land protected by a system of 24 national parks, reserves, and sanctuaries. Conservation groups have also proliferated in recent years.

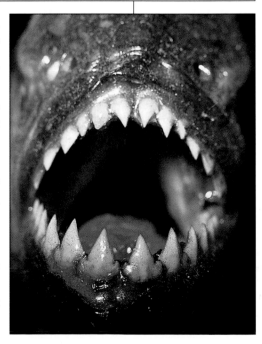

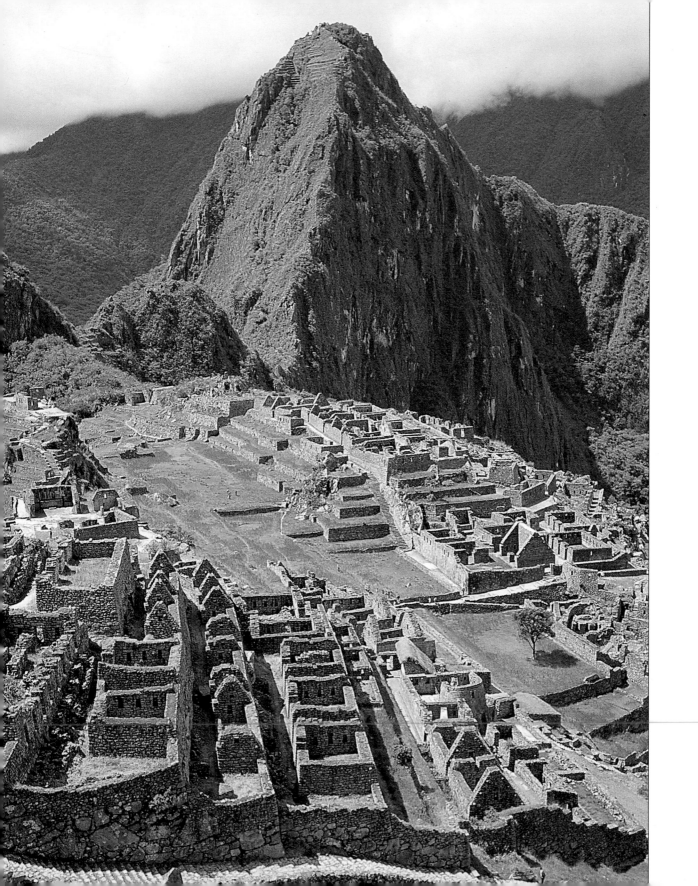

# HISTORY

PERU HAS UNDERGONE MANY CHANGES in its history but has never lost its Incan character. The Incan civilization was the greatest South American empire ever known, even today.

Peru has been ruled by a diverse range of peoples, from the nomadic tribes of the prehistoric period to the city states from which the Incan empire developed.

The Peruvian republic has been in existence for less than 200 years. For 300 years before that, Peru was under Spanish colonial rule. Spanish domination was followed by self-government, but foreign interests continued to dominate the country. Oligarchy, dictatorship, and military coups have plagued its history. Peru has travelled a long road toward democracy from the authoritarianism it has found difficult to shake.

## BEGINNINGS

The first inhabitants of Peru migrated from Asia, crossing the Bering Strait to present-day Alaska, Canada, and the United States. These nomadic tribes moved into South America over successive generations, and some eventually settled in Peru. Around 5000 B.C., communities began to develop, supported by a growth in agriculture. Corn, gourds, and cotton were cultivated in irrigated fields, and the population began to mushroom.

The Chavín culture first united people into a distinct cultural group. From A.D. 200 to 1100, the Mochica and Nazca cultures dominated Peru. Intertribal warfare meant that no empire could last long or extend very far. These cultures were skilled in producing fine ceramics and elaborate metalwork and were adept at weaving complex designs. The Incan culture derived much from these localized tribes and borrowed much in the way of architecture, religion, and art, while establishing the primacy of the sun cult and the Quechua language.

*Opposite*: **Machu Picchu, the "lost city" of the Incas, nestles in the mountains above Cuzco.**

*Above*: **A warlike figure decorates a monument, over 3,500 years old, on the Peruvian coast.**

# THE INCAS

The Incas were originally a small tribe, one of many, whose domain did not extend very far from their capital, Cuzco. They were almost constantly at war with neighboring tribes. About A.D. 1200, they began to expand their rule. Their legends do not predate this time.

The Incan empire expanded rapidly with the reign of the ninth emperor, Pachacuti, from 1438 to 1471. This is about the time that reliable historical records began to be kept, the early rulers being almost mythic. Pachacuti was the most innovative and important of the Incan emperors and is said to have designed and built Cuzco. His first conquest came when his father Emperor Viracocha placed him in charge of the defense of Cuzco against the neighboring Chancas. Not only did he defend the city, but he also overwhelmingly defeated the Chancas, one of the most powerful confederations in the area. This was the start of a mighty conquest.

From 1463 to 1493, Pachacuti and his son Topa Inca expanded the territory north to the present-day border with Colombia and Ecuador and south as far as Chile. The coastline extended 2,500 miles (4,000 kilometers) and encompassed almost 380,000 square miles (1,000,000 square kilometers) of territory with a population of around 16 million.

This realm was linked by a remarkable road system and was administered through a complex bureaucracy that divided labor and land between the state, the gods, and the *ayllus* ("EYE-yoos"), or villages. The empire initiated a massive program of agricultural terracing, to maximize land use, and construction of palaces and temples.

## MACHU PICCHU: REMAINS OF A CIVILIZATION

Hiram Bingham discovered Machu Picchu in 1911 while searching for the ruins of Vilcabamba, the legendary stronghold of the last Incas. Today, it is thought that Machu Picchu is not, in fact, the lost city Bingham thought it was, but it is still not clear what it is. Perhaps it was the center of a rebellious province, or the royal residence of Pachacuti, or the home of the Virgins of the Sun; what is certain is that Machu Picchu was unknown to the Spanish and became lost to Incan memory.

What remains is an astonishing tribute to the architectural skill of the Incas. Situated in a depression high above the Urubamba Valley, these almost intact ruins include temples, houses, even cemeteries, all surrounded by terracing on the mountainsides designed to provide food for the residents. Gradually, other ruins in the area are being excavated, which may help answer the enigma of Machu Picchu.

## THE BEGINNING OF THE END

By the end of the 15th century, the Incan empire was beginning to suffer from overexpansion. Huayna Capac created a new Incan city, Quito, in present-day Ecuador. Preferring this city to the traditional Incan center of Cuzco, he ruled the empire from Quito with his favorite son, Atahualpa, and installed his older son, Huáscar, at Cuzco. In the last year of his life he tried to arrange the division of the empire, ensuring that Atahualpa retained Quito, but this was rejected by Huáscar, the legitimate heir, backed by many Cuzco priests and nobles.

With the sudden death of Huayna Capac in 1527, civil war broke out. Atahualpa, backed by his father's army, was more powerful than Huáscar, and in two major victories defeated his half-brother. At the end of the last battle, in 1532, Atahualpa retired with his army to the hot baths of Cajamarca in the north of the country, hearing strange tales of travelers from afar journeying to meet him.

## THE CONQUEST OF THE INCAS

Spanish interest in Peru began with the discovery of the Pacific Ocean in 1513. Tales about the riches inland brought Francisco Pizarro, a Spanish soldier, to find El Dorado, the mythical City of Gold. In 1528, Pizarro, returning from an expedition to the Caribbean, sought the authority of King Charles V of Spain to conquer the new territory. In 1532, with fewer than 180 Spanish adventurers, Pizarro arrived on Peru's northern coast.

Pizarro and his men set out to make contact with Atahualpa, who had just retired victorious from battle and was resting at Cajamarca with an army of 30,000. Pizarro sent a message asking Atahualpa to come and see him. Because Atahualpa was emperor, Pizarro should have come to see *him*. But Atahualpa came, curious to know more about these strange people. He had an entourage of more than 5,000 and did not believe he could possibly be harmed. Although heavily outnumbered, the Spanish had the element of surprise. They also had guns, cannons, horses (which the Incas had never seen before), armor, and chain mail, which made the Incan wooden weapons useless. They killed most of the Incas and captured Atahualpa.

By capturing Atahualpa and holding him for ransom, Pizarro sent the empire into confusion. The wounds had barely healed from the bitter civil war, and now the state was again leaderless. Atahualpa agreed to the ransom demand and promised to fill a room full of gold and another smaller room twice with silver. Incredulous, the Spanish agreed. Within six months, a room 22 by 18 feet (7 by 5 meters) was filled with gold to a height of 9 feet (3 meters). Gold and silver had been ordered from every corner of the empire, enough to make all the men very wealthy, but Pizarro had no intention of keeping his promise.

A statue of Pizarro in Lima. Pizarro and his men repeatedly tricked their way into the confidence of the Incas only to betray them.

Meanwhile, Atahualpa had been sending secret messages to his nobles in Cuzco, believing that Huáscar was in league with the Spanish. He ordered Huáscar's death. Pizarro's captains became worried by such maneuvers and, pressuring Pizarro, brought Atahualpa to trial in July 1533, where he was given the choice of being burned alive as a pagan or becoming a Christian and being strangled. He was baptized and then killed.

In November 1533, Pizarro went to Cuzco, where he appointed a puppet emperor, Manco Inca, to control the populace. This was the beginning of nearly three centuries of colonial rule.

*Manco Inca, a virtual prisoner of the Spanish in Cuzco, escaped in 1536, raised an army, and besieged Spanish strongholds. He was defeated in 1537 and retired to the mountains, where he resorted to guerrilla warfare until his assassination in 1544.*

## COLONIAL PERU

The consolidation of Spanish control did not run as smoothly as the conquest. Stability was achieved only in 1548, after many internal struggles among the Spanish conquerors, resulting in Pizarro's assassination and Incan uprisings that were bloodily suppressed.

The Spanish established a system called the *encomienda* ("en-koh-MYEN-dah"), whereby allotments of land and natives were given to their men to induce them to stay. This rapidly resulted in serfdom for the native population.

Pizarro founded Lima in 1535, as it made a better transportation center than Cuzco. Wealth was brought from all over the country and then shipped to Spain. In the various regions of Peru, *encomenderos* ("en-koh-men-DER-ohs"), or local chiefs, exacted taxes from villages. For most of the natives, there was no real difference between their old Incan overlords exploiting them and the Spanish. The natives had had little chance to identify with the Incan rulers because of the distance they kept from the people, even to the extent of having a separate elite dialect. The Spanish easily stripped the top layer of power away and took its place.

Pizarro was assassinated in 1541, only nine years after the capture of Atahualpa. He was for a time replaced by the son of his fellow conqueror Diego de Almagro, also named Diego de Almagro. For the next seven years, civil war raged among factions of the conquistadors. Spain, worried at this, sent a viceroy, Blasco Nuñez de Vela, in 1544. He was killed less than two years later. Spanish government forces followed and quickly established control in 1548.

Due to the various diseases that the Europeans brought with them, the native population shrank dramatically. In 1520, there were around 32 million natives in the Incan empire; by 1548, there were five million. The cause was mainly smallpox, aided by other epidemics, such as the bubonic plague, influenza, and measles. A shortage of labor developed, which was remedied by importing slaves from Africa. Over 1,500 black slaves had arrived in Lima alone by 1554.

Spain required more control in Peru than the independent *encomenderos* could provide, so the Spanish government divided the country into *corregimientos* ("kor-REJ-ee-mee-EN-tos"), or units of land governed by a royal administrator. These administrators limited the power of the *encomenderos*, and there was often friction between them.

In 1569, Francisco de Toledo was appointed Peru's fifth viceroy. He wished to reform the colonial system to increase revenue but also to improve the life of the natives, who were increasingly being used as slaves. One of the ways de Toledo improved native life was by resettling people from remote places, where they were easily manipulated by the *encomenderos*, to cities and towns. Most of his reforms stood for many years, but as time went on were subject to abuses.

The 18th century saw the start of uprisings. In Spain, the Hapsburgs were replaced by the Bourbons, who tried to stem corruption in the colonies. This led to rebellion in Peru. With the wave of revolutions over Europe and the Americas in the late 18th century, liberal ideas spread and a sense of national identity arose. The paper *Mercurio Peruano*, first printed in 1790, began to express concepts of Peruvian nationalism.

A painting of the colonial period depicts the marriage of an Incan princess to a Spanish nobleman.

23

**Simón Bolívar, along with José de San Martín, freed Peru from Spanish rule, in spite of the wishes of most Peruvians.**

## *REBELLION AND REPUBLIC*

When Napoleon Bonaparte took control of Spain in 1808, the Spanish colonies were in a state of paralysis. Conflict between those loyal to the deposed Spanish king, Ferdinand VII, and followers of Joseph Bonaparte, whom Napoleon had made ruler of Spain, became a source of agitation for revolution. Peru remained more attached to Spain than its Andean neighbors, and it was only with the arrival of outside forces that Peruvian independence became a reality.

Venezuela and Argentina had already declared their independence, and General José de San Martín, one of the great liberators of South America, had in 1817 freed Chile from Spanish rule. San Martín decided it was necessary to liberate Peru, and in 1820 he landed on Peru's southern coast with 5,000 men. On July 28, 1821, San Martín entered Lima and declared all of Peru a republic.

San Martín devised a constitution that gave freedom to the slaves, abolished native service, proclaimed the descendants of the Incas to be citizens of Peru, and even banned the insulting term "Indian." This constitution frightened many of his supporters into a more conservative frame of mind. San Martín returned home to Chile in 1822, leaving his army in Lima. He sought the help of Simón Bolívar to decisively defeat the royalist armies, offering him the presidency. Bolívar was president of Peru between 1824 and 1826, and royalist troops were finally defeated at the Battle of Ayacucho in 1824. San Martín's promises to abolish native servitude and recognize Quechua as an official language were never kept.

## A TROUBLED BEGINNING

For two decades, there were many internal disputes between the aristocracy and the army. It was only with the presidency of General Ramón Castilla in 1845 that real stability was achieved. Under Castilla, Peru began to seriously exploit its vast and profitable deposits of guano, bird dung used for fertilizer that was found on remote islands. The Castilla administration organized public schools, abolished slavery, and began a railway network to interconnect most of Peru, especially the highlands.

Under Castilla's successors, Peru became increasingly debtridden, and its major export, guano, was exhausted. In 1879, Peru went to war with Chile over valuable nitrate deposits in Peru and Bolivia. The four-year War of the Pacific ended with Peru's loss of the nitrate fields to Chile.

Economically and socially exhausted after the war, Peru was saved from financial ruin only by the intervention of the Peruvian Corporation, a London-based company that assumed responsibility for the enormous national debt in exchange for control over the economy, the railways, the remaining guano, and the untapped rubber reserves in the Amazon Basin.

The ineffectiveness of the presidents who came after Castilla provoked many revolts. Nicolás de Piérola, after heading unsuccessful revolts in 1874 and 1877, finally overthrew the president in 1895. During his administration, Peru adopted the gold standard, and civil marriages were legalized. Here he is shown entering Lima on March 17, 1895.

President Fernando Belaúnde Terry's second term was marked by economic problems and the rise of the terrorist group Sendero Luminoso.

## 20TH CENTURY

Peru entered the 20th century with some stability but was governed by an oligarchy of rich businessmen and landowners. With the presidency of Augusto Leguía y Salcedo, the country rapidly expanded the exploitation of its minerals and agriculture, supported modern industries, and developed its oil reserves. This was made possible by foreign investment, especially from the United States. Lima was modernized with beautiful plazas and parks. But in the rest of the country, especially the Andes, conditions remained unchanged or worsened.

Poor social conditions led to the founding of APRA (*Alianza Popular Revolucionaria Americana*) by Víctor Raúl Haya de la Torre in 1924. This mainly left-wing organization strove to unify the native peoples and eliminate the increasing U.S. influence. After being outlawed for a time, APRA finally won power in 1945 under the presidency of José Luis Bustamante y Rivero. This did not last long, and the Apristas were ousted in a military coup three years later.

## THE COUP OF 1968

During a series of presidencies in the 1950s and 1960s, there was little real reform, especially in agriculture, where it was badly needed. With the election of Fernando Belaúnde Terry in 1963, an ambitious development program was started to exploit the oilfields more fully. But inflation and the urgent need for agrarian reform began to dominate the political agenda, until in 1968 the armed forces again seized control. This military regime embarked on an energetic program of reform. Plantations were turned into peasant cooperatives, and foreign companies and banks were nationalized. But the economy was still a problem. It declined further with the scarcity of fish, partly due to overfishing.

## RECENT HISTORY

After 12 years of military rule, free elections were held and Belaúnde was again elected president in 1980. Discontent with government responses to the needs of the very poor gave rise to *Sendero Luminoso* ("sen-DER-oh loo-mee-NOH-soh," or Shining Path). This Maoist group conducted an ongoing guerrilla war throughout the 1980s, and its terrorist attacks resulted in more than 26,000 deaths.

**Alan García Pérez unilaterally cut payments on Peru's large foreign debt and nationalized banks and insurance companies. His policies eventually led to a period of soaring inflation in the late 1980s.**

In 1985, an APRA candidate, Alan García Pérez, won, but with the rise of terrorism from both left and right, there seemed no resolution to the divisions in Peru.

In the 1990 elections, Mario Vargas Llosa, considered the favorite, was defeated on the second ballot by Alberto Fujimori, the son of a Japanese immigrant. Fujimori instituted a privatization program that reversed the policies of the 1968 coup leaders. He quickly faced opposition from the judiciary, the Roman Catholic Church, organized labor, and the Congress. Congress would not grant him the wide-ranging powers he wanted in order to fight terrorism. Fujimori had cultivated links with the military and with their help staged a coup in April 1992, suspending the constitution and the Congress. In September 1992, the leader and founder of Sendero Luminoso, Abimael Guzmán, was captured, leading to hopes that the guerrilla group's grip on Peru may end.

# GOVERNMENT

IN JULY 1979, Peru adopted a new constitution and the previous one, which dated from 1933, was abolished. The new constitution came into force in 1980 and ended a dozen years of military rule. It was criticized as being too idealistic, expressing political wishes rather than Peruvian realities. Recently changes have been made to the constitution that reflect the growing tension between reality and idealism in Peru.

Under the 1979 constitution, Peru is a unitary republic with independent executive, legislative, and judicial branches of government. For the first time in the nation's history, all citizens aged 18 or over, regardless of literacy, can vote. Voting is obligatory up to the age of 60. A candidate must gain 50% of the vote for direct election to the presidency. Failing this, the top three candidates meet in a runoff election, with coalitions often made.

*Above*: **Current President Alberto Fujimori. Many people voted for Fujimori because he was an outsider who was not associated with the ruling elite that has denied opportunities to many Peruvians.**

*Opposite*: **Troops on parade. The military has played a large role in Peruvian government since independence.**

## THE EXECUTIVE

The president of Peru is the chief of state and commander-in-chief of the armed forces. Elected by popular vote for a term of five years concurrent with Congress and the vice-presidents, the president has the power to submit draft bills, review laws drafted by Congress, and even dissolve Congress under special circumstances.

A premier, chosen by the president, presides over the Council of Ministers (cabinet), also appointed by the president, but it is the president who approves all laws and bills of legislation. The Chamber of Deputies may question and censure the cabinet and its members as well as demand the resignation of a member.

A guard outside a government building in Lima.

## THE LEGISLATURE

The legislative branch of the government is a bicameral congress divided into the Senate and the Chamber of Deputies. The Senate is made up of 60 members elected on a regional basis and includes all former presidents of constitutional governments (as opposed to military dictatorships), who are members for life. The Chamber of Deputies has 180 members elected by proportional representation. In addition to making laws, Congress is responsible for passing the budget and for approving loans and international treaties.

Both bodies of Congress can introduce legislation, but each must allow the other house to revise the work. The president can also review the legislation but cannot veto any law passed by Congress. Congress can also appoint commissions when there is a problem or a concern of national interest.

## THE LEGAL SYSTEM

The 1979 constitution provided for the establishment of a national court of the judiciary, a ministry of justice, and a nine-member constitutional court. It also abolished the death penalty, limited the jurisdiction of military tribunals, and recognized certain human and political rights, including the right to strike.

The structure of the judiciary is designed to be more independent of the government than it was under military law. Judges are appointed by the president from lists compiled by the National Justice Council. Judges are appointed permanently and do not change with the government.

The National Electoral Jury is also independent of the executive. It establishes voting laws, registers parties and their candidates, and supervises elections, which it has the power to void if there are irregularities.

A 16-member Supreme Court, which sits in Lima, is the highest court in the land. Superior courts sit in departmental capitals and hear appeals from lower courts. Courts in the provincial capitals have jurisdiction over all serious crime. Justices of the Peace are the lowest courts and have jurisdiction over petty crime and minor civil matters. These courts are found in nearly all local towns.

An election slogan is painted on a wall in Ollantaytambo.

The military distributing grain to the poor.

## LOCAL GOVERNMENT

The administration of Peru has traditionally been very centralized, and only recently have local governments been given power independent of the national government in Lima. Peru is divided into 25 departments, including the constitutional department of Callao. All departments, except for Callao, are further divided into provinces and subdivided into districts. There are 152 provinces and 1,680 districts.

Each department is governed by a regional assembly. A regional council and a president selected from the assembly act as the executive branch, and the rest of the assembly serves as the legislature. Departments have administrative and economic autonomy. Provinces and districts are governed by locally elected councils and mayors. The size of the council depends on the population of the region. Local officials have the power to administer revenues from local taxes.

Besides these formal governing bodies, there are around 5,000 peasant and native communities, which have a limited form of self-government.

# RECENT EVENTS

One problem with Peru's government is its reliance throughout history on authoritarian leadership and its slight experience with democracy. In 1994, a poll showed that 80% of Peruvians had no party loyalty. Most parties, including Fujimori's, are created specially for a candidate. This has led to instability and attempts throughout the 1980s by terrorist groups like Sendero Luminoso to gain control of remote areas.

On April 5, 1992, after only a few months in office, President Fujimori, with the help of the military, temporarily dissolved Congress. The reason given for this state of emergency (a period when constitutional guarantees are dropped) was the need to combat Sendero Luminoso and other terrorists. Elections were again held in November 1992, and Fujimori won a majority with 44 seats in the new 80-member Congress. The Congress drafted a new constitution, relying on the substance of the 1979 version but granting more power to the executive and especially the president. This constitution was narrowly approved by the electorate (a third abstained) in a referendum in October 1993 that was accompanied by military repression of the opposition. The new constitution, tailored to keep Fujimori in power, overturns the article in the 1979 constitution prohibiting a president from seeking reelection.

Despite the constitutional changes and Fujimori's uncomfortably close links with the military, which still kills members of the opposition, Fujimori is popular because of his crackdown on Sendero Luminoso and his successful economic reforms. Because of this popularity, the opposition has found it difficult to select a candidate for the election in April 1995. At one point even Fujimori's former wife, Susana Higuchi, was set to run against him, disgusted by his alleged corruption.

**The most prominent candidate to come forward so far for the next presidential election has been the former United Nations Secretary-General Javier Pérez de Cuéllar, who announced his candidacy on September 22, 1994.**

33

# ECONOMY

THERE IS AN OLD FRENCH EXPRESSION, "to be as rich as Peru," which suggests how wealthy Peru was once considered. Then, the main exports were gold and silver. Today Peru is a land of extremely rich but unexploited natural resources and also much poverty, unemployment, and underemployment.

Before the coup of 1968, most of the wealth of the country was owned by a very few. In 1968, the government took almost complete control of the economy. Most large firms were nationalized. This alienated foreign banks, and the government found that it had to supply almost half of all investment in the country and to borrow heavily at high rates.

In 1980, a civilian government reintroduced a free market economy. Over the past few years, the Fujimori government has instituted a massive program of privatization of state-owned industries.

*Many state-owned companies are now being sold to foreign companies at a cheap price to encourage future foreign investment.*

*Opposite*: **Vendors sell vegetables at a market in Peru. The country's underground economy forms a substantial part of Peru's economic activity, but does not show up in official figures. Examples include manufacturing facilities in private homes, street vendors, and even a legal system based on verbal commitments.**

*Left:* A sawmill in Pucallpa.

## FACTS AND FIGURES

In 1991, Peru had a Gross Domestic Product (GDP, the total monetary value of all goods and services produced in a country) of $38.2 billion, with an annual growth rate of 2.6%. The average per capita income that year was $1,020. Inflation has risen and fallen dramatically within recent years: in 1988, the annual rate was 667%; in 1989, 3,399%; in 1990, 7,481%! The Fujimori government reduced inflation to 410% in 1991. The economy's annual growth surged in the 1970s but declined with the recession of the 1980s. Inflationary problems hit the economy in the late 1980s, but under Fujimori, economic stability and real growth began again. Although it is not a very industrialized country, Peru has a service sector that contributes almost 40% to the GDP. Imports valued at $3,899 million in 1991 include raw materials, capital goods, consumer goods, and food.

**A textile factory in Arequipa. The unemployment rate in Peru is approximately 10%, but the underemployment rate (those earning less than the minimum wage or working less than 20 hours a week) is around 50%.**

## OIL AND ENERGY

Peru has only recently taken advantage of its petroleum reserves. It began exporting oil in the late 19th century when oilfields were first developed on the north coast. New fields were discovered in the Amazon region, and when the petroleum industry was nationalized in 1968 as Petro-Peru, these new fields began to be developed. A billion-dollar pipeline was completed in 1976 to pipe oil from the jungle over the Andes to the coast. Over 250,000 barrels per day are produced currently, and there are still vast untapped oil reserves within Peru.

More than two-thirds of Peru's energy needs are satisfied by oil and a quarter from hydroelectric plants. The country has coal and gas deposits, but these are difficult to exploit because of the terrain. Shell, an oil company, discovered huge gas deposits, equivalent to nearly two billion barrels of oil, in eastern Peru, but exploiting this resource would require another pipeline around 400 miles (650 kilometers) long, an easy target for terrorists. More promising is the massive potential for a hydroelectric system in Peru because of the Amazon River and its tributaries.

An oil pump on the Peruvian coast. Production of oil has diminished over the past few years but accounts for 5% of Peru's exports.

*Three-fourths of all electricity generated in Peru comes from hydroelectric plants. Peru's water resources have the potential to create 30 times that amount.*

## AGRICULTURE

Although the agricultural sector accounts for less than 14% of Peru's GDP, it employs more than 40% of the population. This distribution of a small amount of production among a large number of people has caused enormous poverty. Almost 80% of agricultural workers are owners of small holdings of less than 12 acres (5 hectares) or are peasants who communally own pasture. Most farmers produce only for themselves, in the same way the native peoples farmed for centuries before the Spanish arrived.

Before 1968, the bulk of the land was divided into large estates owned mainly by a small minority. The 1969 agrarian reform transformed the estates into peasant cooperatives. Altogether 24 million acres (10 million hectares) of agricultural land were expropriated, and 400,000 families benefited. Later in the 1980s, the land was divided into small plots, and more stress was placed on individual enterprise. This policy was not wholly successful, because the land did not usually yield enough.

Agricultural production in Peru is affected by many ills, including outmoded equipment, unpredictable weather, limited arable land, poor organization, and little investment. Poor soil also plays a part, and the diminishing supply of guano traditionally used as fertilizer has resulted in increasing reliance on chemical fertilizers, which are less effective and more environmentally destructive and expensive. For all these reasons, staple foods often have to be imported.

Probably Peru's most valuable crop is the coca leaf, which is refined to make cocaine.

*Below*: **Picking cotton near Ica. Cotton, coffee, and sugarcane are the most important export crops. Potatoes, rice, plantains, and corn are also produced in great quantities but mainly for domestic consumption.**

## WHITE GOLD

To the Incas, coca was known as "the divine plant." Because coca was used in religious festivals and rites to induce ecstasies and visions, it was regarded as a sacred plant. Coca continued to be accepted after the conquest—even the Spanish clergy were enthusiastic about it. Chewing coca leaves (shown below) suppresses hunger, thirst, and tiredness, allowing people to do more work than normal, supposedly double their ordinary workload. The Spanish conquistadors found it vital in manipulating the natives, who were given large quantities of the leaves and literally worked to death in the silver and gold mines. Traditionally coca leaves were used only occasionally, to stave off a shortage of food or the burden of work, and this continues today.

In the 19th century, coca and its more potent derivative, cocaine, were thought to be healthful, especially when made into a tonic or wine. This quickly changed as cocaine became recognized as a powerful, addictive, and deadly drug. In Peru, cocaine is illegal, but coca leaves are not. About 250–500 thousand acres (100–200 thousand hectares) of coca leaves are cultivated for refinement into cocaine, with only 25,000 acres (10,000 hectares) set aside for traditional use. Export earnings from cocaine are $1.3–2.8 billion, most of it profit, because it requires only about $3 million in refining chemicals and leaves to produce $1 billion of cocaine.

Many recent attempts to decrease or destroy the cocaine trade have met with failure. Buying up the crop or substituting different crops have been almost impossible strategies because of the rapid increase in land devoted to coca growing. In the last 10 years, the land used for coca growing has trebled; it could treble again in the near future.

No other crop is anywhere near as profitable as coca. Coca is three times more profitable than cocoa and almost 40 times more profitable than corn. Considering the hard conditions that exist for Peruvian peasants, it is understandable that they are tempted by the possibility of earning many times their normal income by producing coca.

In recent years, the drug trade has become inextricably linked with terrorism. Sendero Luminoso terrorists have forced a partnership on the peasants, protecting growers against government interference in exchange for some of the profits. In an attempt to get rid of Sendero, the military has attempted to ally themselves with the coca growers. This means toleration of the growers while the fight with Sendero Luminoso continues.

**A fishmeal plant near Lima.**

## *FISHING*

For a long time ,Peru did not exploit its long coastline and enormous shoals of fish. Then, from the 1950s to the 1970s, the fishing industry rapidly expanded, to become in 1970 the world's largest, processing around 12,500,000 tons of fish. The main fish was the Peruvian anchovy, which was converted into fishmeal and oil for export. Overfishing and climatic conditions reduced the anchovy catch to 2,800,000 tons in 1991, and fishing is now only for local use.

## *MINING*

Although mining employs less than 2% of the population, it provides over 40% of foreign earnings. The major deposits are copper, lead, and zinc. The inaccessibility of Peru's minerals (most are in the mountains), an inability to buy expensive machinery, the militancy of the miners, and low world prices for metals have all meant that most mineral deposits remain unexploited. In the 1970s, the government nationalized nearly all of the mining industry but did not expand its operations much. Continual losses prompted the government to privatize the industry in 1992.

## EXPORTS

Prior to the 20th century, Peru's main exports were guano and gold. Now almost a quarter of Peru's income comes from exporting raw materials. The country is fortunate in that it produces a variety of exports. This means that it is protected in a recession as it does not depend on one particular item for income. In 1991, Peru's principal exports were copper ($739 million), fishmeal ($467 million), zinc ($324 million), and petroleum ($169 million). The export market was helped by the founding in 1969 of the Andean Pact, an agreement among Bolivia, Chile, Colombia, Ecuador, and Peru to promote the economic integration of the group, eliminate tariff barriers, and settle disputes between the countries.

## TOURISM

Peru is an attractive South American destination for tourists. Peruvians are hospitable, and the country offers much to the tourist in the way of natural beauty, historical sites, and cultural variety. The tourist industry has suffered because of crime, attacks on tourists, and the ever-present terrorist threat. Even so, in a good year the tourist industry can make over $300 million.

# PERUVIANS

PERU IS HOME to an extremely varied group of people. It has the following ethnic mix: whites 15%, mestizos (native-Spanish) 37%, native peoples 45%, and blacks, Polynesians, and Asians 3%.

There has been much intermarriage between the groups over the centuries, and racial classification is difficult, especially because many distinctions are largely a matter of choice. Peruvians define people of mixed Spanish and native ancestry as either *mestizo* ("mes-TEE-zoh") or *cholo* ("CHOH-loh"). Cholos are native people who are attempting to cross over into white society, whereas mestizos are already established. The vagueness of the distinction is a measure of how confusing the ethnic groupings of Peru are. A person may consider himself mestizo while people around him think he is a cholo. These distinctions are not so much racially as culturally defined.

*Opposite:* **A woman from Chincheros in local dress.**

*Above:* **Peru has a young population, with 37% under 15 and only 6% over 60. Figures show a gradual slowing down in the growth rate, making the population stable, unlike most other South American countries. Population stability is one of the first signs of an emerging economy.**

## POPULATION FACTS AND FIGURES

The population of Peru is approximately 23 million. About 70% of Peruvians live in urban areas, a figure that reflects increased migration to the cities in the last two decades.

The average life expectancy is 65 years. Although the country is strongly Roman Catholic, a religion that forbids artificial birth control, the annual growth rate is only 2.1%. Over 50% of married women of childbearing age use contraception. Families are often larger than North American families, with four to seven children being the norm.

A fair Peruvian, such as the one above, is not necessarily elite, because the term refers to a class based on wealth and position, as well as ancestry.

## SOCIAL CLASSES

The Spanish conquerors established a class system based on race: a white upper class that ruled a lower class of Indians. In the 20th century, a middle class of mestizos developed. Today, most people remain in the class they were born into; education is the main chance of advancement.

The coastal and Sierra regions have quite different elite, middle, and lower classes, the urbanization of the coast having produced totally different social conditions from the rural Sierra.

**THE ELITE**  The coastal elite, numbering only a small percentage of the total population, spring from a variety of sources: members of the agricultural aristocracy, successful immigrants or their children, and the Peruvian representatives of foreign business. Descendents from the old Spanish families form one of the largest parts of the elite.

The elites' wealth can be based on banking, finance, marketing, land ownership, or industry. Until the military coup of 1968, 44 families dominated Peruvian affairs in nearly every sphere. This small number of people owned a substantial amount of the land, estimated at more than 70% of the country. The military dictatorship, which was mainly middle-class and mestizo, stripped these families of some of their wealth, but the redistribution still went mainly to the top 25% of the people.

Most of the elite live in Lima and Callao, and less often Trujillo and Arequipa. Those who live in the Sierra have declined in significance as their power in local government and agriculture has been eroded. Estates

A middle-class family in Cuzco: both parents are teachers. Middle-class occupations include doctors, teachers, professors, lawyers, small business persons, shop owners, the military, and government employees.

were divided by inheritance laws and families became less influential, until in 1969 nearly all land holdings were taken from them.

One of the main ways the elite on the coast retained their privileges was by not relying on their private estates for wealth but by diversifying into business and finance. They have also used kinship bonds to incorporate the newly rich into their society and strengthen ties with other families.

**THE MIDDLE CLASS** Only around 15–17% of Peruvians are middle class. Like the elite, the middle class is mainly urban, educated, and Spanish-speaking. It looks to the elite for its values. At one time, over half the middle class was employed by the government.

The middle class in the Sierra is wholly dependent on cheap native labor and is itself in the employ of the elite, looking after their estates and filling local government and administrative posts.

In postwar Peru, and particularly during the period of military dictatorship, a new middle class developed that relied on its expertise rather than depending on the elite for employment. Because of recent political events and the diminishing power of the elite, the middle class is now taking the lead in the creation of a new Peru.

## IMMIGRANTS

Until independence, Peru was not open to immigration, and the only foreign arrivals were a few African slaves imported to work on plantations. Foreigners began arriving in Peru in the 1830s. Compared to Brazil or Argentina, immigration was not on a large scale and was usually work-related. Chinese immigrants came between 1850 and 1875 to work on the railroads and guano deposits. (The

picture shows a lion dance in Lima's Chinatown.) Many Japanese arrived in Peru in the early 20th century, and today around 20,000 people of Japanese descent live in Lima, including President Fujimori. In the business community, the British and North Americans are the biggest groups, but there is also a small number of Europeans and Arabs. The neighboring countries of Colombia, Chile, Bolivia, and Ecuador have contributed around 20,000 residents.

*Above*: **A Chinese lion dance on parade.**

*Below*: **A slum in Lima.**

**THE LOWER CLASS**  The lower class is highly diverse, covering nearly 80% of the population. It includes the unemployed, laborers, small farmers, small shopkeepers, itinerant traders, and artists, in addition to servants and enlisted personnel.

Because of this diversity, the lower class has great difficulty in forming an organized front or creating a union powerful enough to take on the bosses. Farm laborers have little in common with small farm owners. Even the highly skilled union members find it more advantageous to make alliances with the middle-class professional unions.

The family is one of the most important aspects of life for the lower class. Marriages in the Sierra, however, are more stable than those in the coastal areas. Parental authority is also more evident in the Sierra than in the coastal region.

Families get together and organize entertainment, fiestas, soccer games, and dances that the whole community enjoys. Associations springing from family ties also try to organize political and economic activities, pressuring politicians and local landowners.

## NATIVE PEOPLES

The native peoples can be subdivided into two groups, those from the Andes region and those from the Selva.

**THE ANDEAN NATIVES** The central and southern Andes are populated by the Aymará and the Quechua. The Quechua live mainly in the Sierra departments of Ancash, Ayacucho, and Cuzco. Several other departments also have a high proportion of Quechua speakers: Junín, Huánuco, Huancavelica, and Apurímac. The Aymará are found mainly in the southern departments of Arequipa, Moquegua, and Tacna. Because of migration in the 20th century, substantial numbers of both native groups now live in the cities, especially Lima.

The Aymará and Quechua live side by side, although there is little marriage between them. The Aymará are likely to speak Quechua as a second language, the Quechua, Spanish. They both hold stereotyped views of each other: the Aymará consider the Quechua old-fashioned,

The faces of these Andean men recall the features of the Incas.

*Cholos provide an important link between the natives and national institutions, enabling them to influence the national, political, and social agendas.*

A native woman from Tinqui with her daughter. In a 1970s reform, natives were renamed peasants instead of Indians, as the term *Indian* was considered insulting. At one stage, it was even illegal to use the word *Indian* in reference to the Aymará or Quechua people.

uneducated, and lazy, whereas the Quechua think the Aymará stubborn, argumentative, and money-minded.

Mestizos and whites make no distinction when it comes to natives: they consider all of them disgusting. A popular Sierra saying goes, "The Indian is the animal closest to man." The native is almost universally despised by Peruvians, who hold them to be inferior, drunken, superstitious, dirty, lazy, and addicted to coca. After all the reforms made by the military regime in the 1970s, the natives are still dislocated from the rest of the country, not just because of their languages but because of these stereotypes about them. Some native families who have risen socially go to great lengths to hide their native origins.

There is a great deal of social mobility between the natives and mestizos. The natives only need to adopt Spanish as their main language, don Western rather than traditional clothing, and take up a mestizo occupation. The people who do attempt this are called cholos. It is often an insulting term, suggesting that the person is trying to rise above his or her proper place.

**THE AMAZON NATIVES** A much more diverse collection of tribes lives east of the Andes in the Amazon basin. Although there are only around 200,000 natives in the Peruvian Amazon, they belong to 53 different ethnic groups, speaking 12 main languages and many varied dialects. Some tribes have only a handful of members left, whereas others, like the Jívaro with 8,000 members and the Campa with 21,000, are doing very well.

The Amazonian peoples have a fierce and warlike reputation. The Incas, although powerful builders of an empire, could not subdue them, and there are many legends of hordes of Amazons repeatedly sacking Cuzco. Generally, the Incas left these people alone, except to trade with them in cloth, bronze, axes, exotic fruits, and wood. When the Spanish arrived, they were confronted with various tribes who would not accept their authority. Expeditions into the jungle ended in Spanish annihilation.

One of the fiercest and most interesting Amazon tribes still thriving today is the Jívaro. The Jívaro live in the wet tropical forest to the east of the Andes. Despite attempts to conquer them, they retain their homeland.

The Jívaro fish and hunt monkeys and birds with blowguns and poison darts. They keep domestic animals, gather berries and roots from the forest, and plant banana trees and manioc. Cloth is woven by the men on small handlooms and made into skirts something like a kilt; this is worn by men and women. Chiefs and shamans wear feathers denoting their status. Each small white bone on the left shoulder of a warrior represents a man he has killed. Women usually wear robes pinned on one shoulder, but some people wear ponchos.

Family life revolves around the house, which can hold 30 to 40 relatives. Polygamy is common because of the shortage of men due to warfare, mostly

A Jívaro man. Like most tribes, the Jívaro take hallucinogenic drugs to see into the supernatural world and give them the courage to face death in battle.

between different Jívaro communities.

The Campa, to the east of the Andes, are similar to the Jívaro in not having been conquered by either the Spanish or the Incas. They are also similar in repulsing missionaries, especially those who seek to impose monogamy. By 1800, the Campa were left in peace. Although as hostile and resistant to invasion as the Jívaro, they have had to put up with settlers occupying their land.

Clothing is made from jungle materials—bark cloth is reddened with dye and worn like a robe. Men and boys hunt pigs, deer, and monkeys, and fish for food. Traditionally agriculture was considered women's work. Women grew bananas, yucca, sugarcane, and coca.

The Campa have much more contact with the outside world than the Jívaro, and this influences their culture. Occasionally a tribe can minimize the damage done to their culture by outside influences. The Shipibo of central Peru, who live along the Ucayali River, have retained their cultural identity although historically they have had many links with outsiders. They even have a cooperative where they sell their pottery and weavings to museums and shops around the world.

The Amazonians have also had problems with terrorists. In 1990, Sendero Luminoso killed the Ashanika chief. In retaliation, the Ashanika drove all the guerrillas from their land.

*Opposite:* **Yagua Amazonians wearing their usual dress.**

*Below:* **A house in the Selva. The homes of the Campa are often without walls and consist of a palm-thatched roof supported by poles.**

## CONFLICT WITH THE SPANISH

The Jívaro are fairly representative of the history of tribes in the Amazon area. The Spanish tried to establish towns in their jungle area because the land contained much gold, but they were greedy in trying to tax the Jívaro too much. This led, in 1599, to a massive rebellion, with the Jívaro killing 20,000–30,000 Spanish, burning and sacking their towns. They captured the Spanish governor and subjected him to cruel tortures in retaliation for his increasing tax demands. They melted down gold and poured it down his throat until his bowels burst, saying they wanted to see whether he could get his fill of gold. But even though they could deter the Spanish, they could not withstand the diseases the Spanish brought. The natives retreated farther and farther into the interior, and the Spanish left them alone, except for the unsuccessful attempts of missionaries.

For several hundred years, there was peace, and then in the 19th century, the boom in rubber brought the rubber barons and their guns. Whole villages were destroyed by the rubber barons, who enslaved the remaining population. If any tribe or village was known to be particularly hostile, the barons surrounded the village and slaughtered its inhabitants. After 1912, however, the rubber market collapsed worldwide, and the natives were left alone again.

In the 1960s, however, the government settled highland peasants into the Amazon and opened the area for the exploitation of its hardwoods and petroleum. In the early 20th century, nearly 40 tribes had never been contacted by outsiders; today there are probably only two or three.

# MIGRATION

The poorer you are in Peru, the more likely you are to migrate. Those who migrate, either temporarily or permanently, do so from the Sierra to the coast, and from the rural to the urban areas. At the beginning of this century, Sierra natives were recruited for the coastal plantations and mines. Generally this has changed; the towns and cities have now become the main focus of migration. More rarely, Serranos may go to the Selva for the harvest season because the tropical harvest time is during the Sierra off-season.

Mestizos are different from the indigenous people in that they tend to migrate from towns in the Sierra to towns on the coast. Theirs is usually a permanent or long-term migration. With the elite, migration is less common because most of the people of this class reside on the coast. But with the erosion of the elite's dominance in the Sierra, due to government land redistribution, some members of the elite have retired to the coast where their children have taken jobs in the service sector, such as television or finance.

Earlier in the century, the coastal mines or plantations were the main destinations of migrants, but from the 1960s onward Lima has been the main target. It is a cumulative process—Serranos move to Lima because relatives or friends are there. Over the years, associations and clubs have sprung up to organize migrants, helping them get jobs and housing. The housing has usually been in squatter camps called *pueblo jóvenes* ("PWEB-loh HOE-ven-es"), or small towns. As a community, the settlers arrange their own services until the local government helps them. Despite poor wages and very basic housing, many migrants still have better services and wages on the coast than in the Sierra.

Migration has helped to change the lot of the poorest classes in Peru by putting them in touch with a larger society that they have little contact with in the Sierra. Natives who come to the coast frequently learn Spanish, become literate, join unions, vote, and gain experience with a cash economy, rather than the barter system. When these migrants return to the Sierra, they bring with them the skills to deal with the outside world and to negotiate with local employers and plantation owners. They also become the intermediaries in the community through whom the native Serranos can articulate their wishes.

## CLOTHES MAKE THE PERSON

People who live in the cities and towns and mestizos who live in rural areas wear Western dress. Traditional dress is much more frequently worn by natives in the rural areas.

The Spanish changed every aspect of native life when they came to Peru. This included introducing new materials such as sheep's wool (the Incas used alpaca wool) and silk. Tailoring was also introduced. During the 1570s and 1580s and after the native revolts of the late 18th century, the Spanish issued edicts forbidding the wearing of traditional clothes, which was a sign of nationalism to the Spanish. By around 1700 a native man with high social status would wear European-style clothing, whereas the women persisted in wearing Inca-style dress.

**NATIVE MEN'S DRESS** Contemporary native dress is a mixture of Spanish and Inca. A native man's pants and shirt are European. The shirt, called *kutun* ("KOO-tun"), is made of wool or cotton and usually factory-made or made by local market tailors. The pants, or *pantalones* ("pan-tah-LO-nes"), are made from handwoven wool cloth of one color, usually black, which is called a *bayeta* ("bay-YET-ah"). A *bayeta* vest or waistcoat is sometimes worn over the shirt, called a *chaleco* ("cha-LEH-koh"). Sandals are made either of tire rubber or leather and if not made in the home can be found in most markets.

Each village has different patterns or colors associated with it that are reproduced on the costumes, and this applies to hats as well. Brimmed hats called *monteras* ("mon-TEH-rahs") are very common and worn by natives and cholos. The style is reminiscent of Spanish colonial hats. More traditional, and sometimes even worn underneath the *montera*, is the *chullo* ("CHOO-yoh"), a handknit hat with ear flaps. It is usually brightly colored and can be decorated with buttons. Originally the *chullo* came from the Aymará people, but now it can be seen all over the highlands.

## PONCHOS

Originally from Chile, the *poncho* was introduced in Peru during the 17th century. Ponchos are made of two pieces of cloth woven from alpaca or sheep's wool, with a hole left in the middle for the head.

Every locality has an individual poncho style, with distinctive colors, motifs, and patterns. Elaborate patterns have been developed over the last 400 years. Inca designs survive in geometric patterns and in the use of llamas, birds, and men; the Spanish introduced horses, butterflies, and the double-headed bird—the Hapsburg eagle.

It has been estimated that the time it takes to spin, dye, and weave a traditional poncho is around 500–600 hours over a period of up to six months. Because of this, one poncho is generally given to a person on entering adulthood and is expected to last a lifetime.

Aymará dancers during wedding festivities. One of the most interesting sights in the highlands is the brightly colored bowler hats some natives wear. Adapted from the British bowler hat around 1900, they have become a favorite with natives. The colors denote the wearer's locality.

**NATIVE WOMEN'S DRESS** Women braid their hair into two strands, which are then tied together at the back. Like the men, they wear a *montera* and sandals. The skirt, or *pollera* ("po-YEH-rah"), is a full-gathered wool skirt, usually with a decorated hem. Traditionally they are black, but they can be found in navy blue, pink, yellow, or orange. On festival days, a woman will wear as many *pollera* as possible to signify her wealth. Most women own only one or two. Around Cuzco, a short jacket, or *saco* ("SAH-koh"), which is ornamented with braid and buttons, is worn. The belt is the same as a man's.

A *manta* is worn by nearly every woman and is a rectangular or square piece of handwoven cloth. If a village has a particular color or design on its ponchos, it usually repeats the design on the *manta*. To keep the *manta* in place, a *tupo* ("TOO-poh"), or small pin, is used. This has a flat, hammered, circular head with knife-sharp edges. The pins can vary in design and be in the shape of flowers or birds and trees. Depending on what class the woman belongs to, the pin can be made of copper, silver, or gold. Also commonly used is the safety pin.

# LIFESTYLE

PERUVIANS TODAY find themselves in the midst of a rapidly changing society. In the past three decades, economic upheavals together with developments in transportation and communications have had a profound effect on the lives of many Peruvians. Old ways are disappearing or being adapted to new influences. Changes in the roles of women and the growth of the middle class have had their effect. The growth of public education is bringing new opportunities to the native peoples. But Peruvians have long experience in adapting to changing influences; under the domination of the Incas and later of the Spanish, Peru's people learned to resist and renew themselves under adverse conditions. Once again, they are in the process of resisting and renewing.

*Opposite:* **A Shipibo from the Amazon basin carves a musical instrument. The Shipibo have retained much of their traditional culture.**

*Left:* **A couple waiting to be married in Cuzco.**

A girl helps her mother unload a donkey-load of onions in Cuzco.

## *ROLES OF WOMEN AND MEN*

Peru is generally a man's world, and the Hispanic concept of *machismo* ("ma-CHEES-moh"), which defines masculine attributes and the firm belief in male superiority, is paramount. Machismo is a point of distinction for a South American male. It evokes the image of someone who is strong and respected, in addition to being protective and providing well for his wife and family. There is a constant double standard in the treatment of men and women. Whereas men may have a mistress or lover, women are strictly forbidden to do this. Whereas a man can divorce his wife because of her adultery, a woman generally cannot do the same unless there is a public scandal.

As it is a Hispanic concept, machismo is not practiced by the native peoples. The Quechua still practice trial marriage, where women and men choose their partners and can end the relationship when they wish. The woman is free to enter another marriage with no stigma attached to her. Any children resulting from the union are regarded as belonging to the community as a whole.

Although the 1993 constitution guarantees the equality of women and provides laws that do not discriminate against them, women still face traditional barriers deriving from machismo that impede their social and business prospects. In general Peruvian men still maintain that a woman's place is in the home, cooking and cleaning and looking after the family. If she has to take a job to supplement the family income, she must also take care of the work in the home.

A man with his child. Not all Peruvian men conform to traditional roles.

According to statistics, the female share of the labor force has changed little over the last two decades. In 1970, women were 20% of the work force and in 1992, this share had risen to 24%. However, many of the jobs held by women, such as in street stalls or informal employment, are not reflected in these statistics. Faced with the economic crisis of the 1980s, many women have been forced to supplement the family income by working part-time or setting up street vendors' stalls. Middle-class women have started their own businesses or entered professional careers.

The feminist movement is relatively new to Peru. It is essentially a movement belonging to well-educated, middle-class urban women, and most organizations have a left-wing bias that deters elite women from joining. Most of these groups are restricted to helping urban women by providing legal and educational ways to improve the treatment of women. A recent survey showed that 94% of the women in the department of San Martín had been battered at some stage by men. It was also asserted that there were 35 rapes per month in that department. Due to the fear of further retaliation, women frequently do not report crimes against them. Police suspect that only 10% of crimes against women are reported.

*Flora Tristan, the daughter of a Peruvian noble, is an important figure in 19th century French letters. A renowned feminist and socialist, she advocated free love, divorce, and the abolition of slavery in her* Pérégrinations d'une paria.

A Quechua wedding. By the time a couple marries, they may have several children, who cannot be baptized until their parents are married.

## FAMILY

The family is the most important social unit in Peru and forms the center of the community. An adult who is not married is unusual and is not accepted into the community. There is little regular visiting between people who are not kin.

There are regional and socioeconomic differences, but a household of several siblings and their respective spouses is usually the basic domestic unit. Usually children live with their family until they marry and even afterwards as well. Young men and women from upper-middle- and upper-class families sometimes get their own apartments before they are married, but it is commoner for newlyweds to live with their large families until enough is saved to set up house for themselves. Individuals in these families may own separate belongings, but generally the house and land are of common ownership and land is farmed together if in a rural environment.

The family cycle begins with the marriage. The arrangement can be very flexible for some in the lower classes and the Quechua. Often an alliance between a couple is arranged by their parents, but it is initiated because of the couple's choice. Next they enter a period of *sirvinakuy* ("seer-veen-ah-KEE"), meaning "to serve each other," during which the woman works with her mother-in-law and the man with his father-in-law. This is a test of their readiness for marriage. During this stage they may sleep together under the same roof, usually with the man's family. The

couple generally do not marry until a child is conceived, showing the union to be fruitful, and even then might postpone the wedding for a long time. Weddings are frequently ornate and expensive occasions and can take years to finance.

A patriarchal system exists within the family, where the father is the head of the household. Young men achieve independence from their father only gradually over a period of years. Even among brothers, the eldest takes precedence. Boys generally inherit from their fathers and girls from their mothers. As the parents grow older, they gradually loosen their authoritative hold on the family.

Migration to urban areas can weaken the ties of rural families, making them less complete and less extended. The migrants are also cut off from a family base. To compensate for this isolation, they move to places where relatives have previously migrated.

Because race is so important in terms of class and socioeconomic position, family background or a good family name is one of the key aspects of life. Families descended from the 16th century Spanish settlers are more than proud of this fact. If the family has a crest or coat of arms, this is proudly displayed above the door of their home.

**In Peru, family means more than just the immediate family and includes a wide kinship circle of several generations. A typical couple is likely to have between three and six children.**

It causes great concern when patronage is introduced into public services and government. The current Fujimori government has a cabinet containing several old friends of the president. Patronage in government can lead to widespread corruption and inefficiency. As civil service jobs are usually for life, this leads to no meaningful change.
With the recent privatization of public industries and services, President Fujimori has tried to lift this burden from the state.

## PATRONAGE

Hispanic countries have a tradition of strong, tight-knit families, and Peru is no exception. In the world of business, this is often extended so that family members are incorporated into firms that may be family-run or publicly owned. This action is called patronage, and although in North America such nepotism is not considered appropriate, in Peru it is seen to be perfectly reasonable.

One of the principal reasons for patronage is that an employer who selects family members for the job knows the strengths and weaknesses of the persons he or she is hiring, having often known them all their lives and perhaps their parents as well. The employer can thus fit them into jobs that suit their skills accurately. The employer can also trust family members more than strangers, and the employees in return work to the best of their ability out of family loyalty. It is considered unthinkable for an employer when hiring to look outside his or her family or for somebody not intimately known.

In some ways, the system of patronage is detrimental to business because it can prevent new blood and ideas from entering a firm. It can dissuade more talented people who are not family members from making a positive contribution to the family. Few positions of importance will ever be given to non-family members.

## GODPARENTS

Social life revolves around the family, and its importance is paramount. To offset this influence and connect the family with the outside world, *compadres* ("kom-PAH-drays"), or godparents, are chosen for children for the major religious and social events in their lives. Baptism, the first haircut, and marriage are the main events for which *compadres* are chosen. A child might have several sets of godparents during his or her life, but the most important are those chosen for baptism. Although originally a Hispanic custom, having godparents is also practiced by the native peoples.

Depending on the region in which they live, godparents' duties vary, but generally when their godchildren are baptized, gifts are given to the parents and children and a contribution is made to a fiesta, if one is held.

Godparents are meant to give a good start in life to their godchildren. As a godchild grows up, godparents are less obliged to help unless the child is in serious trouble. It is meant to be a lifelong relationship of great love and respect. Sometimes when a godchild is orphaned, he or she is raised by a godparent. Social and emotional ties are created, and the serious obligations of the godparent are paid back by the child's love and respect.

People within or outside the family can be chosen as godparents, but generally it is better for a well-off person, a hacienda owner, boss, or prominent mestizo to be chosen. In the native community, this links the family to the wider community and society outside. For the poor, it acknowledges their dependence on the rich, and this in turn obliges the rich to better their lot.

Godchildren call their godfather *padrino* ("pah-DREE-no") and their godmother *madrina* ("mah-DREE-nah"), and the parents of the children call the godparents *compadre* ("com-PAH-dray") and *comadre* ("com-MAH-dray") respectively. These affectionate names indicate the closeness of the relationship both for the children and for their parents.

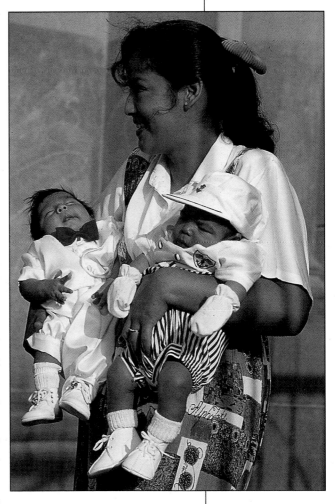

**A double baptism. Children generally receive godparents at their baptism.**

63

*Everybody knows his or her place and status within a Peruvian family. Roles are clearly defined, and the behavior appropriate to the person's status is expected at all times.*

## ROLES WITHIN THE FAMILY

At the top of the pyramid is the father, who is the authority in the household. He expects his wife to be obedient and attentive to his wishes. In return, he shields his wife and children from harm or social disgrace. He must maintain the good name of the family.

The Peruvian woman has to be many things: a good wife, a mother, and a hostess. She manages the affairs of the household, not just cooking and cleaning, but also entertaining visitors or her husband's clients or employers. In upper-class, families a wife who performs these difficult duties with style and grace is considered a real asset to her husband's career. But society and her husband consider a wife's main duty to be that of looking after the children, educating them morally and socially. (In the picture, a woman teaches her daughter to weave.)

Only recently have women of the upper class been allowed to work for money rather than the usual volunteer work for charities. In the lower classes, financial strains force women to seek employment.

# HEALTH

The health of Peruvians is generally improving, although health care is disproportionately weighted toward the coast and Lima and government aid is minimal. The government health program receives 2.4% of the national budget, down from 6% in the 1970s, although the economy has grown over the last two decades.

Peru's public health system faces major problems. A survey in 1990 showed that only 53% of the total population has access to drinking water: 73% of those in urban areas and 18% in rural areas. The five principal causes of death have remained unchanged over the years. In descending order of occurrence, they are: influenza and pneumonia, intestinal infections, diseases of the heart, perinatal conditions (sickness arising before and after birth), and malignant tumors. The infant mortality rate has halved over the past 25 years, although it still ranks as the fourth largest cause of death. In 1970, 108 babies in a thousand died, whereas in 1992 the figure had dropped to 52.

A fundamental health problem in Peru is malnutrition. The per-capita supply of food has decreased since the 1960s to around one-half to two-thirds of the calories a person needs. Add to this poor sanitation, with less than half of the urban areas and 1% of the rural areas having sewers, and there is a potential breeding ground for disease. Despite this, average life expectancy has increased by 10 years in the last two decades and is now 65 years.

Malnutrition is one of the main causes of the high infant mortality rate; 11% of all newborns are underweight because of the mother's malnutrition.

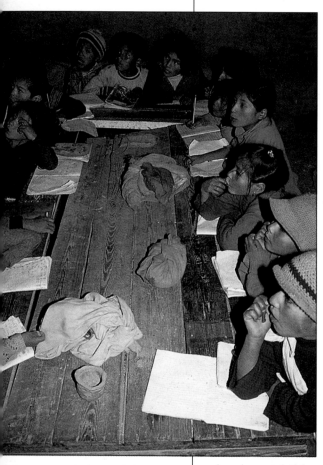

**Schoolchildren in an isolated Andean village near Cuzco.**

## *EDUCATION*

A good economy comes from a well-educated work force. A 1970 survey showed Peru ranking sixth among South American countries in terms of the percentage of the population reached by education. The top five countries all did better economically. Education in Peru has expanded dramatically in the 20th century, but formal education still faces tremendous problems.

After half a century of debate but little action, a General Law of Education (1972) sought to reform an unequal education system in which much of the population, especially native peoples, were excluded from education. Improvements have been brought about by the 1972 legislation.

The ratio of teachers has increased from the 1970 figure of 35 pupils per teacher in primary schools to 28 in 1990. The percentage of students enrolled in school has also increased. For primary education, around 70% of primary school-age children were enrolled in 1970, but nearly 90% were enrolled in 1990. In secondary education in 1970, 31% of secondary school-age children were enrolled, whereas in 1990 the figure had jumped to 70%. For college education, the figure was 19% in 1970 and 36% in 1990. Adult illiteracy is down from 27.5% in 1972 to 14.9% in 1990 (8.5% men and 21.3% women). In the latest budget, the government has not shown its commitment to education, however, allocating only 3.5% of the budget to education, down from 6–7% in the 1970s.

Below the age of 6, preschool day care is provided, and there are programs for those who do not attend day-care centers. These programs run parallel with education for parents on nutrition and child development.

Rather than have specific age-related education, the Peruvian system breaks down basic education into three cycles, with students proceeding to the next cycle on completion of the previous one. Education is obligatory from ages 6 to 15, during which time students should be able to complete their basic education. In practice, however, only approximately 12% of children who begin basic education finish it.

In rural areas, teaching is in the native language, usually Quechua or Aymará, in the early years. Spanish is taught in the upper grades. Many of the children in Peru live in remote areas far from schools, so to provide an education for them a system of *núcleos* ("NOO-klay-ohs") was developed. *Núcleos* are scattered throughout the country and serve the needs of several nearby communities. They are not as big as schools but can teach all three cycles of the basic education program.

A field in the Urubamba Valley. Village life is hard and simple, with most villagers surviving on subsistence agriculture. Each family grows just enough food to live on for the next year. If the crops fail, there can be serious difficulty.

# A VILLAGE IN THE ANDES

The road to a typical village in the Andes is usually narrow and made of earth, baked hard in the summer and muddy from torrents of rain in the winter. A network of narrow roads runs over the mountains connecting small, isolated villages, but in bad weather they can be totally cut off. Old buses and heavy trucks use these roads, in addition to pack animals, such as llamas.

A field in the Urubamba Valley. Village life is hard and simple, with most villagers surviving on subsistence agriculture. Each family grows just enough food to live on for the next year. If the crops fail, there can be serious difficulty.

At the end of the road, the village is mainly inhabited by Quechua who have lived in the same way for a thousand years, in much the way as Europeans lived in the Middle Ages. The few concessions to modern living are Western dress, running water (still rare), metal pots and pans, radios, and flashlights. Crops and livestock introduced by the Spanish have also been adopted.

Electricity is rare—only big villages have a generator. A village is more likely to have drinking water from a few taps dotted throughout the village. If not, people have to trek to the nearest stream or spring several times a day to carry water back. Houses are usually made of earthen bricks baked in the sun, or in rare cases, stone. The floors are made of hardened earth, roofs are thatched, and cooking is done in a hearth in the center of the floor. The houses are often smoky from the hearth fire, and the undersides of roofs are black and sooty. There is little furniture beyond a stool or two. A comparatively wealthy

*Reducciones were laid out according to a special plan. The right site was picked for the town, at the right altitude, near a stream or spring, with enough room to build a church, a cobbled main street, and at least one official building. Each family's house had a door facing the street so that the family could be observed and monitored.*

family might have a locally made, rough-hewn bed or table. The bed is usually a pallet covered with blankets and sheepskins. In a prosperous home there might be a bed frame with a mattress of bundled reeds. Women squat on the floor; men sit on benches made from earth. Families own very few personal items: clothing, pots and pans, tools and farming implements, their house, a little land, and most importantly, the radio.

The crops a village grows depends on the altitude of the village. A village high in the mountains grows potatoes and a few grains and keeps herds of llamas, sheep, goats, and, if they are relatively wealthy, some cattle. On the lower levels, lemons, limes, avocados, and chilies are cultivated in addition to ordinary vegetables.

Towns or large villages in the highlands are often the result of a policy pursued by the Spanish Viceroy Francisco de Toledo in the 1570s. The Spanish gathered together all the native peasants living in scattered communities and put them into one town in order to control and tax them more efficiently. The policy was called *reducciones* ("ray-duc-SYO-nays"), which means reductions. After some years of living in these artificially created towns, the natives often went back to their old homes.

## A DAY IN THE ANDES

The woman of the house is the first to rise, stirring last night's embers into a fire and then putting on the kettle to brew some *mate* ("MAH-tay"), a sort of herbal tea. At breakfast, which is around dawn, *mate* is served to the family with either bread or *mote* ("MOH-tay"), boiled dried corn.

As the family eats breakfast, the mother prepares lunch, or *almuerzo* ("al-MWER-zo"), which is eaten when most people in North America would be eating their breakfast. *Almuerzo* consists of a thick broth of potatoes and other vegetables, a hot sauce made of chilies, and a mug of *chicha* ("CHEE-chah"), a beer made of fermented corn. This meal is served to all the workers in the household. These might include fathers, sons, and grandfathers. There may also be *compadres*, godparents of their children, or just neighbors who owe the family a day's work in return for working on their fields. After eating, the men go to work in the fields.

When the men have left, the woman begins to prepare the third meal of the day, which is more complex and plentiful than the other two. It includes two or three dishes with the usual potatoes and *mote*, but with the addition of meat in special thanks to the men helping her family. If the job the men are carrying out in the field is a communal one, the woman may be assisted in her task by the wives or mothers of the field hands. She is also expected to look after the children, milk the cow, lead it to pasture, and feed the chickens and pigs.

By around noon, she packs up the meal with all the utensils, plates, spoons, and maybe a bottle or two of *trago* ("TRAH-goh"), a cane liquor, and *chicha*. The burden is shared with the other women, who also come with her to the fields. The children accompany them unless an older child is left to look after the young ones.

The men eat and drink, and as they return to work, the women will either sit and watch, drinking *chicha* and playing with the children, or they will work in the fields themselves, plowing, hoeing, or reaping. At the end of the day, which is usually twilight, everything is gathered up and they go home. Cattle, sheep, or goats are herded up and taken back also. At home, they drink a last cup of *chicha* before the beds are laid out. The fire is reduced to a few glowing embers that will light tomorrow's kindling, and the family goes to bed.

The people in the Andes begin their day to the sound of the radio. There are over 550 radio stations in Peru, but the one the highlanders listen to is Radio Tawantinsuyu, where DJs speak in Quechua and folk music begins the day. For people who live in a remote village and go to a small market town only once a month or twice a year, a radio is almost a magical connection with the rest of a very strange, foreign world.

**A native woman prepares food in a traditional Inca-style house in the Andes.**

# RELIGION

ALTHOUGH PERU DOES NOT HAVE AN OFFICIAL RELIGION, most people in the country consider themselves Catholic. For the native peoples, however, Catholicism incorporates much of the former Incan religious beliefs. The majestic mountains that surround them are considered to have spirits, offerings are still made to the earth, and images of the sun still figure prominently in religious iconography. For the people of the Andes, Incan beliefs and Catholic doctrine have fused into a harmonious whole in which the festival of St. John the Baptist conveniently coincides with the old Incan festival for the winter solstice and traditional marriage customs naturally accommodate a church wedding.

## ANCIENT PERUVIAN BELIEFS

The religion of the ancient Incas permeated all aspects of public and private life. They worshiped many gods, goddesses, and spirits, each of whom was responsible for a different aspect of life.

Viracocha was the most important god, having created the sun, moon, stars, earth, oceans, and weather—in fact, all natural things. Like many Incan gods, Viracocha is neither male nor female, nor just one person. The god's complexity is apparent in his/her responsibility both for water and fire.

Illapa represented thunderbolts, lightning,

73

The sun god had the most elaborate temple in ancient Cuzco. Its walls were covered in gold and silver plate, and solid gold statues adorned its halls. Sacrifices and rites often took place here, as well as at the temples of Viracocha and Illapa. Rituals were intended to placate the gods and ward off cataclysms. Sacrifices were made of birds, llamas, guinea pigs, coca, corn, and sometimes people, although this was rare and reserved for times of great suffering.

*The Incas inherited aspects of earlier religions as well as beliefs from newly conquered regions, but they superimposed their own brand of mysticism on them. This helped conquered peoples adapt because they were able to keep their own gods while admitting the superiority of Viracocha and the sun.*

rain, hail, snow, and frost. Venerated mainly in the highlands, Illapa, his son, and his brother were depicted as the deities of the mountains.

The god Pachacamac ruled over the lowlands and the underworld, causing earthquakes and pestilence. He was represented as a golden fox. Amaru was a serpent who rose from the underworld, symbolizing the communication between the living and the dead.

Some deities were exclusively female; these included Quila, the moon, who was the wife of the sun. Statues of her were made of silver, and those of the sun were of gold. Quila was associated with the earth and death.

The center of the Incan religion was undoubtedly the sun god. Although not as powerful as Viracocha, the sun was more physical and less mystical. The emperors of Cuzco demanded to be recognized as direct descendants of the sun, which gave them a semidivine status and an excuse for military subjugation of other regions. The sun reigned over the highlands (considered the center of the empire) and the heavens. He was a paternalistic god who planned for the welfare of the universe and its people, the Incas, while controlling their every action.

## THE NAZCA LINES

The Nazca Lines, giant drawings in a desert in the south of Peru, were created by the Nazca people between A.D. 0 and A.D. 600. The lines cover such a wide area that they are only properly visible from the air. A variety of animals are represented: a 600-foot (180-meter) lizard, a 300-foot (90-meter) monkey with a tightly curled tail, and a condor with a 400-foot (120-meter) wingspan. The picture below shows the hummingbird. They were created by removing the top layer of earth to  reveal the lighter-colored dust beneath. Other designs include triangles, rectangles, or straight lines that run across the desert, sometimes for more than a mile. There are several dozen different figures.

Maria Reiche, shown above, has devoted her life to studying the lines. Her theory—that the lines were intended for the gods—is now the most widely accepted explanation. Based on the constellations, the lines would have reminded the gods of the needs of the Nazca. Reiche speculates, for instance, that the drawing of the monkey, the Nazca symbol for the Big Dipper and their representation of rain, was created during a drought to remind the gods that the earth needed rain.

*Now nearly 90 years old and blinded by glaucoma, Maria Reiche has enlisted U.S. astronomer Phyllis Pitluga to continue her work. Since 1946, when she began to study the lines, Reiche has taken only one short break from the work that has made her a national hero in Peru.*

The Cathedral of Lima sits on the site chosen by Pizarro, but has been reconstructed several times after earthquakes.

## THE ROMAN CATHOLIC CHURCH

Peru is almost exclusively Catholic, with less than 3% of the country professing another religion. Around 300,000 are Protestants, 20,000 are Baha'is, 6,000 are Jews, and 6,000 are Buddhists, mostly immigrants from Japan. The total number belonging to other religions is virtually negligible. Often Catholicism is combined with native myths and legends. Catholic festivals were usually substituted for the Incan religious festivals on the same date, so the two inevitably became mixed. Incan religion and other native religions linger on in the mountains and jungles.

The history and destiny of Peru have been profoundly shaped by the Catholic Church. The Church reached Peru with Francisco Pizzaro in 1533, and only a few years later, in 1537, the diocese of Cuzco was established. The Church quickly founded hospitals, including a 12-room hospital in Lima for natives, and schools. Almost 60 schools were established by 1548, and in 1551 the University of San Marcos in Lima was created.

Schools were a part of the Church's program of conversion of the natives, which started immediately with the Spanish arrival. Many obstacles made this conversion difficult, including the varied forms of local cults and the size of the native population, which was widely spread over an inhospitable terrain.

Although they were the prime target of conversion, native peoples were excluded from becoming priests until the 17th century. Mestizos and Creoles made up the majority of the clergy. Foreign priests from Spain and the rest of Latin America have often been needed because of a gradual decline in the number of priests since the 19th century. Even quite recently, in 1963, 70% of bishops were foreign. In 1821, there was one priest for every 500 people. Today, there is one priest for every 8,000 people.

The 17th century was known as "the religious century." The Church was at the pinnacle of the artistic and intellectual culture it had helped to create. Many sculptures, paintings, and the grand colonial cathedrals were all made at the behest of the Church. Two saints were also canonized during this period, the most famous being St. Rose of Lima (1586–1617). She was the first saint to be canonized in the Americas, and her

**The altar of San Pedro Church in Lima.**

sympathy for the native peoples made her the originator of social services in Peru. Another Peruvian saint, St. Martín de Porres (1579–1639) was the first black saint and became the patron saint of interracial justice and harmony for the civil rights movement in the United States.

## *CHURCH AND STATE*

The Church in Peru has always been involved in social matters, which has occasionally conflicted with the state's interest. Formerly priests often told people how they ought to vote. During the campaign for independence in the 1800s, the clergy (mainly consisting of mestizos) supported the revolutionaries against the Spanish.

**Peruvian soldiers carry a saint's litter in a procession.**

In 1845, Catholicism was made the official state religion. Foreigners were allowed to conduct their own services, but no Peruvians were allowed to attend. The 1920 constitution gave individuals freedom of religion, which was subsequently reaffirmed in the 1979 constitution. In the constitution of 1933 and in amendments made in 1940 and 1961, the state declared that the country was no longer officially or formally Catholic. Despite this, the Church was given special status, and religious instruction is still obligatory in all educational institutions in the country.

Although it has been one of the more conservative churches in Latin America, the Peruvian Church has increasingly supported socially progressive movements and proposed reforms. The military coup of 1968 was supported by the Church because of the military's agrarian policy, which nationalized most property. The coup unleashed a reborn dedication to social reform, which is presently doing much to alleviate the condition of the peasants. This has meant criticizing the present government. A side effect has been an increase in the Church's popularity with the poor. When Pope John Paul II visited in 1985, vast public rallies were held in celebration.

The Church is such a large and varied institution in Peru that at times it can appear to be both critical and supportive of the government because different factions within the Church have differing views. Opposition to the Church has come from both the right and the left, the government and military as well as Sendero Luminoso. The Church's social projects have been destroyed, and priests have been killed by both sides.

## TWO REMARKABLE SAINTS

Peru is the birthplace of two saints of particular importance to the Americas: Santa Rosa of Lima and San Martín de Porres.

San Martín de Porres was born in Lima in 1579, the illegitimate son of a noble Spaniard and a black woman. It was not customary at that time to allow a mulatto to enter a religious order in Peru, but because of his exceptional qualities and virtue he was admitted to the Dominican Order in 1610. Martín was known for his kindness to all people, especially to the poor and the unfortunate. He was also a special friend to animals. He established an asylum and a school for the youth of Lima, which is considered his monument. His feast day is November 5.

Santa Rosa of Lima was the first person born in the New World to be canonized by the Catholic Church and is called the patron saint of the Americas and the Philippines. She was born in Lima in 1586. Although her mother wanted her to marry, Rosa was determined to devote her life to her religion, and in 1606 her mother relented and Rosa became a nun, living in seclusion in a hut on the family property. Her feast day is August 30.

*The Peruvian Catholic Church in the last few decades has made special efforts to reach the people. Masses are delivered in Quechua, Aymará, and other dialects. In Villa El Salvador, a shanty town south of Lima, Father Eugene Kirk, an Irish priest, says, "Many don't understand Quechua, but they are so dumbfounded a foreigner speaks it that they reconsider their parents' language. There is a perpetual process of re-evaluation."*

Catholicism is still influential with the lower classes, and the parish is still the center of the community.

# MODERN RELIGIOUS PRACTICE

Although Peru is overwhelmingly Catholic, people generally display only nominal allegiance to the Church. A mere 20% of the population attend mass regularly. Most people practice "popular Catholicism," which means attending occasionally for special events like the sacraments, festivals, processions, or saints' days. Among the middle and upper classes, religion is losing its importance. Some are alienated by the Church's newfound extremism.

Fiestas celebrating saints' days or religious holidays are an important aspect of community life. They act as a break in the routine of hard work. Each family in the peasant community takes turns paying for the fiesta of that year, usually at great personal expense.

The Church has done much to integrate Spanish and Incan beliefs. Spanish Catholic festivals usually replaced Incan ones, but remnants of Incan belief still exist. In the Sierra, old traditions abound, and people who act as healers talk with spirits to diagnose diseases and offer herbal medicines.

# SHAMANISM: MAGIC AND CURE

Shamanism has been popular for over 3,000 years. Because Peru is a developing country and most of the people cannot afford or obtain doctors, many people, especially the natives and the poor, rely on the ancient healing art of the shaman or *curandero* ("kur-ahn-DAIR-oh," or healer). Even former President Belaúnde's family employed one. The shaman can be found in every large community, principally in the Sierra and the Selva. People may travel hundreds of miles to see one. The tribes of the Amazon region have best maintained the shamanistic culture and spiritual traditions.

Shamanism uses herbs and therapy to cure people not just from physical sickness but from fear, jealousy, tension, and anger. The treatment draws on the combined spiritual and magical elements of native culture. It attempts to treat the entire life rather than just the symptoms.

Most shamans use hallucinogens (potent drugs extracted from plants) once used by the Incas. Under the influence of the hallucinogen, the patient goes through a period of revelation, during which the shaman asks the person questions and sets tasks, the meaning of which will reveal the source of the person's illness. Shamans also take the drug in order to see into the future, recover lost souls, and find lost objects. Sometimes the whole community participates. Traditional spirit-songs are then sung, and the experience provides a way of getting in touch with the spirit world of the ancestors. This heals the discordances of modern life and the encroaching industrial world. The shaman acts as a conserving force against this encroachment, preserving the culture of the tribe as established by their ancestors. Below is a shaman ceremony at the Inti Raymi festival.

# LANGUAGE

WITH THE SPANISH CONQUEST in the 16th century, the Spanish language quickly rose to prominence in Peru. Native peoples were accustomed to having rulers who spoke a different language. In fact, the Spanish conquest was helped by the fact that the Incan emperors and their court at Cuzco spoke a different language from their subjects, who thus felt little allegiance to them.

Today, Spanish is the official language of Peru. People of the highlands generally speak Quechua or Aymará, and the native peoples of the Amazon region speak languages from 12 different linguistic families. There is also Creole slang. Linguistically varied and used at all levels of society, Creole slang is a result of the rich mixture of cultural influences Peru has undergone.

## NATIVE LANGUAGES

Aymará is a regional language with few speakers, most of whom live around the southernmost part of Peru adjacent to Lake Titicaca. In comparison, many natives still speak Quechua, the ancient language of the Incas. It is popularly known to the native peoples as *Runasimi* ("Mouth of the People"). During the days of the Incan empire, it was spoken in the region that is modern-day Peru, Bolivia, Ecuador, and parts of Argentina and Chile. It continued to spread after the Spanish invasion, but its use has now diminished to the confines of Peru and parts of Ecuador and Bolivia.

There are around 10 million speakers of Quechua, with the highest density in the south. Many are from the Andean highlands. It is the largest indigenous language to survive in the Americas and has given some words to the English language: *llama, cóndor, puma*, and *pampa*, among others.

Quechua has many regional varieties, a result of the immensity of the old Incan empire, which encompassed many different peoples. The purest

*The word "Indian" is regarded as an insult. The Spanish word* indígena *is used instead.*

*Opposite:* **Two Quechua men greet each other at a wedding.**

**83**

**Most Quechua speakers can also speak Spanish, although around 25% speak only Quechua.**

and most prestigious form of Quechua is now spoken around Cuzco, the former capital of the Incas.

For a long time, Quechua was seen as a backward language or a language of subversion. It was outlawed by the Spanish in 1780 after a peasant revolt, and it was even discouraged by Simón Bolívar. Despite this, it survived. For a time in the 1970s it even became the "official" language of Peru. This was quickly watered down; official recognition remains only in areas where it is widely spoken.

The Incas did not have a written language and had no alphabet. Instead they had *quipu* ("KEE-poo"), an elaborate system of knotted string. This simple system was effective in communicating complex pieces of information (including detailed censuses) used in administering a large empire.

During the 16th century, the Spanish clergy tried to learn Quechua, both to record the past history of the Incas and to convert the natives by translating the Bible. They wrote Quechua in the Roman alphabet, and it has been written this way ever since. The first book printed in Peru was a catechism in Quechua for the use of priests in teaching the natives.

## SOME BASIC WORDS IN SPANISH AND QUECHUA

|    | SPANISH        | QUECHUA        |
|----|----------------|----------------|
| 1  | uno            | hoq            |
| 2  | dos            | iskay          |
| 3  | tres           | kinsa          |
| 4  | cuatro         | tawa           |
| 5  | cinco          | pisqa          |
| 6  | seis           | soqta          |
| 7  | siete          | qanchis        |
| 8  | ocho           | pusaq          |
| 9  | nueve          | isqon          |
| 10 | diez           | chunka         |
|    |                |                |
| good morning | buenos días | wenos dias |
| good evening | buenas noches | wenas nuchis |
| yes | sí | ari |
| no | no | manan |
| hello | ¡hola! | napaykullayki! |
| please | por favor | allichu |
| thank you | muchas gracias | yusulpayki |

*Nearly all the countries in Latin America use Spanish as their official or main language, with the most important exception of Brazil, where Portuguese is spoken. Including the population of Spain and Spanish speakers in North America, there are more than 300 million people worldwide who speak Spanish. Spanish is one of the easiest romance languages to learn. It is spoken as it is written, and many words are similar to English. The word order is also similar. In addition, Spanish in Latin America is spoken much more slowly than the Spanish in Spain.*

A young couple talking in the park.

*Peruvians are very open and friendly, and it is no surprise to see women walking arm in arm with other women or men with men.*

## GREETINGS AND GESTURES

Men and women shake hands when meeting and parting. Men embrace close friends or pat them on the back. Women kiss one another on the cheek. When two women are introduced, they may kiss one another. The same is sometimes true of men and women. Elders and officials are greeted with their title and last name. Principal titles are *Doctor*, *Profesor*, *Arquitecto* ("ahr-kee-TEC-toh," architect), and *Ingeniero* ("een-hain-YER-oh," engineer). Some Peruvians call foreigners *gringo* if a man or *gringa* if a woman. In Peru this is a normal form of address.

People discuss family and occupation when meeting someone. To rush in and talk about business is considered rude. Some topics of conversation can be difficult. Because of the recent political situation in Peru, politics can be a very touchy area. Another is a person's ancestry. Most Peruvians feel more comfortable being associated with their Spanish colonial background rather than their native heritage.

When Peruvians talk to one another, they stand much closer than people in the United States, and to back away is taken as an insult. To beckon to someone, Peruvians wave their hand back and forth while holding it vertically, palm facing out.

# THE PRESS

Freedom of the media is guaranteed by the 1979 constitution. This upholds the right to information, opinion, expression, and dissemination of thought in any form and through any medium without prior authorization

or censorship. But Peru has suffered from a long history of interference by various political groups. In 1974, the Peruvian press was nationalized, which immediately stopped critical reporting about the government. The military government sought to reduce external cultural influences and promote the national culture and education. The papers returned to private ownership in 1980, but the previous six years of government control had devalued newspaper companies both in deteriorating machinery and low circulation. In 1981, Congress introduced legislation providing for compensation, yet this did not prevent subsequent political pressures. With escalating political violence in the 1980s, civilian governments again put pressure on the press to refrain from supporting terrorism, even excluding references to terrorism. In 1990, the Fujimori government closed *El Diario,* considering it a supporter of Sendero Luminoso. Between 1983 and 1991, numerous journalists have been killed, 17 by government security forces.

Around 45 papers are published in Peru. Most big cities in Peru have a daily newspaper. Because of the high level of illiteracy (15% of people cannot read or write) and distribution problems, papers are mainly restricted to the Lima area and other main cities.

# ARTS

PERU HAS MANY CULTURES. Thousands of years before Europeans arrived, New World civilizations came and went in the area that is now Peru. Over the centuries, many civilizations contributed to a diverse and thriving culture. Racial and geographic factors have produced a regionalism in the arts: the natives of the Amazon retain their cultural independence, the urbanized coast is greatly influenced by Europe, whereas the Sierra still preserves the flavor of the Incan empire. Probably the only area of artistic expression that is shared by all of Peru's people is the art inspired by the Catholic Church.

## NATIVE AND SPANISH: TWO SEPARATE ARTS

Peru's artistic achievements fall into four periods: pre-Incan, Incan, colonial, and postcolonial. There was little disruption between the pre-Incan and Incan periods, but colonization brought increasing tension and division in the artistic world between the traditional native cultures and the new. The Spanish conquerors destroyed much of the artwork created by the Incas. Nearly all of the metalwork done in gold or silver was melted down. The Spanish imposed their own culture, destroying native art and traditions. For centuries after the conquest, the arts were little more than a direct imitation of Spanish styles. Ironically, native artisans were often employed by the Church to carve statues and decorate interiors.

After independence from Spain, Creoles tried to forge a new artistic culture distinct from the Spanish but were reluctant to revert to the native culture. They began to look toward the whole of Europe rather than just to Spain. It was only in the early 20th century that Peruvians began to appreciate the indigenous past and their artistic heritage. European influence and the indigenous past have remained two separate artistic strands, often conflicting in 20th century Peru.

*Opposite*: **Textiles in Pisac. In some communities, the men weave.**

*Below*: **A pre-Columbian textile from the Paracas necropolis culture, around A.D. 400–800. By this time, almost every technique known to the Andean weaver had already been invented.**

# FROM POTTERY TO PAINTING

Some of the earliest remains of visual art in Peru are to be found in the pottery and weaving ancient cultures left. Many different civilizations, the Chavín, Paracas, Nazca, Chimu, and Mochica, to name a few, developed new techniques and styles that they passed on to the next culture. The designs and colors from the pottery and textiles of ancient civilizations are still used to this day and made in a similar way. Their bright colors and inspired ornamentation make modern masonry and architecture seem dull in comparison. Motifs typically included many fishes, reptiles, birds, and mammals. The Mochica culture introduced the representation of everyday human experience: children playing, someone with a toothache, women washing, and lots of portraits.

**Pottery from the Mochica culture of A.D. 300–1000.**

Military expansion facilitated the spread of artistic styles, so that with the rise of the Incan empire, artistic styles became universalized. The Incas incorporated many earlier designs in their work and spread these throughout their empire.

With the coming of the Spanish, painting with oils on canvas and fresco painting were introduced. Churches and monasteries required decorations and paintings: these were imported from Spain. Soon European painters arrived, especially from Italy. One of the first was Bernardo Bitti, who emigrated to Peru in 1548.

In the later 19th century, artists began to rediscover their native past. The *costumbrista* ("kos-toom-BREE-stah") movement made the everyday life of the native peoples the subject of art. Painters such as José Sebogal tried to create a national school based on native themes.

In the 20th century, visual artists divided into two schools: the *indigenistas* ("een-dee-hain-EES-tahs"), who follow the native culture and style, and the *hispanistas* ("ees-pan-EES-tahs"), who draw on the Spanish heritage. Some Peruvian artists have tried to combine the two. Fernando de Szyszlo is the best recent artist to include native motifs in his abstract painting. Ricardo Grau and Macedonia de la Torre reflect the traditions of their country while blending them with modern European styles.

Peru's most famous modern sculptor, Roca Rey, works in metals and has held exhibitions all over the world. His work is exhibited in various museums in the United States and Lima.

## THE BRILLIANCE OF INCAN GOLDSMITHS

The quantity of gold to come from Peru in the 16th century was colossal, and most of it was in the form of art objects that the Spanish melted down into ingots. The chronicler Garcilaso de la Vega describes the Emperor Atahualpa's gardens as including life-sized imitations of corn, flowers, and

animals, all made in gold and silver. Whole buildings and courts were sheathed in plates of gold. Yet nothing, no matter how beautiful, was spared by the Spanish. The examples that survive today are extremely rare and come from remote regions of the Incan empire or from looted graves. Gold was a sacred element symbolic of power to the Incas and thus often used as a tribute to the emperor or buried with nobles. Items buried included images of gods, cups, jewelry, and ornaments.

The tools used to make these objects, which often had quite intricate patterns, were crude, consisting mainly of stone hammers, chisels, and wood and stone rollers for smoothing. Decorative techniques included incising, stamping, scratching, and inlaying with precious metals and gems such as turquoise, amber, emeralds, and silver. The astounding craftsmanship visible in the artwork preserved in Peru's museums today makes one understand the high social standing accorded to craft workers in Incan times.

## *ARCHITECTURE*

Before the Incas, buildings were constructed mainly of mud and straw with some use of wood. Even today many poor people live in mud and straw houses. The artistry of the Incas is visible in their architecture. Incan architecture is technically very accomplished, as can be seen in structures like the walls in Cuzco and the city of Machu Picchu. Massive blocks of rock were crafted with stone or bronze tools, smoothed off with sand, and then dragged up and down the many steep mountains of Peru using human strength alone. The Incas covered the walls of their dwellings with gold; decorations, statues, and ornaments filled the alcoves.

With the arrival of the Spanish, a new style of architecture sprang up, which included new buildings, such as churches and monasteries. The Spanish relied on native workers and materials, but they created a very Spanish style. Mansions in Lima were replicas of Andalusian mansions. Also evident are the Moorish origins of the Spanish style.

Native influences slowly began to seep into architectural style and decorations. Incan motifs, such as the sun and pumas, can often be found in church friezes. This native style can be seen in many buildings in the more remote areas, especially Puno and Cajamarca.

*One of the most ornate churches in Peru is La Compañía in Lima, which has a magnificent baroque facade and rivals the city's cathedral in its splendor.*

## MUSIC AND DANCE

Peru's music does not fit into one category. The multitude of different regions, histories, ethnicities, and classes has ensured a wide variety of sounds.

The most famous Peruvian music is the Andean folk music originally played in the highlands. Sad songs are mixed with whooping, energetic ones, and all are done to a communal and stylized dance.

Andean folk music dates back to the ancient civilizations of Peru. Clay panpipes have been found in ancient graveyards on the coast. The Incas used a variety of flutes and panpipes, conch-shell trumpets, and drums made from puma skin. The Spanish introduced string instruments, which the native musicians adapted. Some uniquely Andean instruments are the

**Musicians playing in a courtyard. The most popular music in Peru, Andean folk music is easily found in music halls or *peñas* ("PAY-nyahs"), especially during festival time.**

*churrango* ("choo-RAHN-go"), a kind of mandolin using an armadillo shell as a sound box, and the Andean harp. Other standard instruments in folk bands are cane flutes, panpipes, and drums.

*Peñas,* or nightclubs, can be smart and chic or untidy and primitive, but either way they are home to *criolla* ("cree-OH-yah"), or Creole, music. Spanish guitars and percussion blend music from many sources, African to European, to create an often slow, romantic form with love ballads. There are regional variations with their own accompanying dances.

*Chicha* music, named after the beer, developed in Colombia. It is faster than *criolla* and mixes saucy lyrics with energetic percussion and electric guitar backing. *Chicha* can often be heard in the highlands but is based mainly in the jungle, where it is played at many Saturday night fiestas.

A style that shows the diversity of Peruvian music is *música negra* ("MOO-see-kah NAY-grah," or black music). This style originated in the old slave communities on the coast. The music is linked to social protest and portrays daily life in the communities.

## *LITERATURE*

The written word is relatively recent in Peruvian history. The Incas had no system of writing, although literature abounded in myths and legends that were passed on orally. The Spanish conquest brought the first pieces of national literature, mainly historical and descriptive pieces discussing the nature of the conquest. The *Royal Commentaries of the Incas*, written in the 16th century just after the conquest by Garcilaso de la Vega, a half-Spanish half-Incan noble, is a fascinating document providing many insights into the preconquest world of the Incas.

It is in the 20th century that Peruvian writing has come into its own. In the centuries before this, Peruvian writers had reflected the tastes and forms of Spanish literature. The internationally renowned poet César Vallejo was one of the first of a generation of poets, artists, and writers to attempt to free himself from European influence and produce a distinct culture, even though he lived abroad for many years. It is the fate of many of Peru's modern artists, poets, writers, and intellectuals that they still have to go abroad to discover what is unique about their own country. Through a trial of foreign influences, they become more aware of their country's individuality. Problems of cultural identity and an interest in the Incan heritage are the main themes of Vallejo and his contemporaries.

Peru has also produced a good crop of modern novelists in addition to the famous Mario Vargas Llosa (nicknamed "Super Mario"). Less known but equally important are Ciro Alegría, whose *Broad and Alien Is the World* describes life in the Sierra, and Manuel Scorza, whose *Drums for Runas*, written in the style of the South American magic realist school, deals with the struggles of the miners in the highlands.

José María Arguedas is uncommon among Peruvian writers because he writes solely for and about the native peoples.

*Peru has provided inspiration to both native and foreign writers. Thornton Wilder wrote* The Bridge of San Luis Rey *from an old Peruvian romance he once heard. The fishing villages of Peru's northern coast probably inspired the creation of Hemingway's* The Old Man and the Sea.

# MARIO VARGAS LLOSA—A WRITER IN POLITICS

Mario Vargas Llosa is Peru's most famous intellectual and novelist. He first achieved fame in the 1960s when the Mexican Carlos Fuentes and the Colombian Gabriel García Márquez also came to prominence. Like most Latin American writers, Vargas Llosa has also been active in politics.

With over 10 novels, four plays, an abundance of essays, and the first part of his autobiography, *A Fish in the Water*, Vargas Llosa is a prolific author. Born to an affluent family in Arequipa in 1936, he was sent away to school at the Military College in Lima at the age of 10. His first novel, *The Time of the Hero*, deals with the effects of the college's cruel and authoritarian regime upon its pupils. The military in Peru burned the book.

Vargas Llosa is very much a stylist, concentrating on the form and narrative structure of his novels. *Conversations in the Cathedral* is an example of this complexity, a multilayered text profiling corruption and power in the Lima of the 1950s.

Although a native Peruvian, Vargas Llosa has spent many years abroad, mostly in Europe, returning only to spend the summer months at his coastal home near Lima. However, he retained a keen interest in Peruvian politics, his views changing as he grew older. Starting on the radical left in the 1960s, he gradually moved to the right. Disagreeing with the nationalization of the banks in 1987, he joined a new right-wing political party called *Libertad* (Freedom), which later became the Democratic Front. With their help, he began his bid for the presidency, espousing a radical, free-market economic program that would privatize all of Peru's state companies.

The writer who had written so sensitively about his own country was not the politician who entered the 1990 presidential race. Vargas Llosa seemed very remote from the problems of the Peruvian poor. On a second ballot, he was beaten by Alberto Fujimori. A few days later Vargas Llosa flew to London. He became a Spanish citizen and now lives in London.

*"Peru is for me a kind of incurable disease and my feeling for her is intense, bitter, and full of the violence that characterizes passion."*

—*Mario Vargas Llosa*

# LEISURE

MOST PERUVIANS LEAD A DIFFICULT LIFE, with little time for leisure activities. In the rural areas, women may spend leisure moments knitting or doing other small tasks around the house. Men may take a leisurely meal or spend some time drinking *chicha*. Otherwise, the time to relax is during *fiestas*, when everyone spends the day (or the week) dancing, eating, and partying.

City dwellers are likely to take a trip to the beach or go to a movie. (U.S. film distributors have been so successful in Peru that the government frequently requires cinemas to show Peruvian films and documentaries.) A favorite pastime is to spend the evening in a *peña*—lively nightclubs with colorful performances—dancing, listening to Creole music, and enjoying beer and *ceviche*, a popular seafood. Barranco, a suburb of Lima, is particularly well known for its *peñas*.

*Opposite:* **Women knitting in Puno. Women frequently use their leisure hours for relaxing work such as knitting.**

*Left:* **Young people playing volleyball on Uros Island in Lake Titicaca. Peru's women's volleyball team has had great international success.**

A bullfight near Cuzco. Pizarro brought the first fighting bulls to Lima, holding the first bullfight in 1538. Many years later, in 1768, a permanent bullring was built in Lima. It is the third oldest bullring in the world after the ones in Madrid and Seville. Before construction of the bullring, the main town square was used. In rural areas, fields are often used as the arena for contests.

# LA CORRIDA

Bullfighting (*corrida,* "koh-REE-dah")) is extremely popular in Peru. Wealthy families breed bulls at their haciendas, encouraging the animals' ferocity and speed and sponsoring fights in Lima. The best matadors are invited from as far afield as Venezuela, Mexico, and Spain and offered up to $30,000 for an afternoon's sport. The bullfighting season starts in mid-October on the day of the Lord of the Miracles festival and continues until Christmas. There are usually eight fights held each Sunday during this time.

After an opening parade and some initial testing of the bull, the *picadores* ("pee-kah-DOR-ays") enter on horseback, stabbing the bull's shoulders with lances to weaken its neck muscles. They are followed by the *banderilleros* ("ban-duh-ree-YER-ohs"), who insert 20-inch (50 cm) darts into the bull's neck to weaken it further. The brightly colored ribbons of the darts continue to flutter as the bull charges around.

The last act of the drama now begins with the entrance of the matador. The matador maneuvers his *muleta* ("moo-LAY-tah," a piece of red cloth) to tease the bull in preparation for the kill.

After the correct number of passes, the matador kills the bull. The most difficult and dangerous method is *recibiendo* ("ray-see-BYEN-doh"), where the matador stands directly in front of the bull and thrusts the sword between its horns as it charges. The extreme danger of this technique is heightened by the rule that the matador cannot move his feet until the bull is dead. The more usual technique is *volapié* ("vohl-ah-PYAY"), where the matador runs around the charging bull and stabs it between the shoulder blades. If the kill is successful, the bull dies instantly and the crowd cheers. If it is merely wounded, the crowd may scream obscenities and throw rubbish at the hapless matador.

The occasional matador on horseback distinguishes Peruvian bullfighting from that in other countries. The *paso* horse was developed just for this purpose and is extremely agile in dealing with the unpredictable bull.

*At one period in Peruvian bullfighting, the lance and sword were completely dispensed with, leaving the horseman just with his cape, his courage, and the bull.*

**A rural bullfight attended by churchgoers after mass.**

101

## SPORTS

Sports have always been a good way of bringing a community together, and in small villages, the after-work focus of life is often the local soccer team. Sports have been popular since early times. The Incas played versions of badminton and basketball, which can be seen illustrated on ancient vases. Today soccer is the favorite sport, although there are also many baseball and basketball teams. Pool and tenpin bowling are also available. Many country clubs offer golf, swimming, and tennis. Volleyball (there has been a women's Olympic team) and polo also have a large following and even the English game of cricket is played at the Lima Cricket Club. But these are the sports of the rich, and recreation facilities are much more plentiful in the cities than in the country.

## WATER SPORTS

The village of Ancón, north of Lima, used to be an old fishing village but has in this century become the international playground of the rich who wish to fish and sail their yachts. The Cabo Blanco is a famous and exclusive fishing club in the village. Ernest Hemingway visited there, and today yachting is a popular pastime, with many sailing to the Galapagos Islands. Deep-sea fishing is popular all along the western coast, where the catch includes black marlin, flounder, sea bass, snook, corvina, and mackerel. In the Andean lakes, fly-fishing for trout is extremely popular, and many tourists come from Europe and the United States for this sport.

**City dwellers, especially in Lima, like nothing better on the weekend than a trip to the beach.**

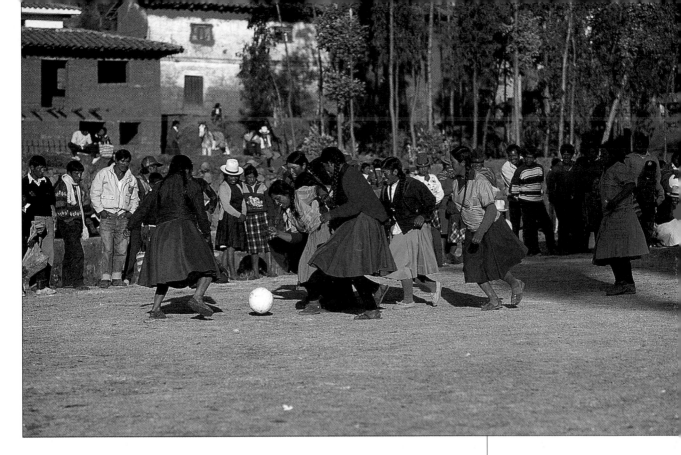

## BEACHES

The most fashionable and famous beaches are very close to Lima—almost, in fact, in its suburbs. Limeños flock to Costa Verde in the thousands on Sundays, and the beach is often filled to capacity. The resorts farther south are better for swimming, particularly Paracas National Park, a peninsula of great natural beauty near Pisco.

## SOCCER

Soccer, called *fútbol*, is the national sport of Peru. The National Stadium in Lima is the location of the most important soccer matches and other events. The national team qualified for the 1992 World Cup in Madrid but could not qualify in 1994. Soccer was first played here in 1892. It was introduced by British emigrants, and the first club was founded in 1897, with leagues starting in 1912. The seriousness with which the sport is taken is shown by the incident in May 1964, when rioting killed nearly 300 people in Lima after Argentina scored a last-minute goal to beat Peru.

**Watching cockfights is a favorite pastime in Peru.**

## *HORSERACING*

Horseracing is a popular spectator sport, and races are held most weekends and some weekday evenings in the summer. The hippodrome in Lima is the focus of Peruvian horseracing, with races most evenings except Monday. Racing is mainly for the moderately wealthy and town dwellers. In April, Lima's National Concourse celebrates Peru's famous pacing horses where high society comes to see dressage competitions.

## *COCKFIGHTING*

Cockfighting, on the other hand, is very much the sport of the poor. Trained cocks are placed face to face in a pit or on a stage and let loose to fight each other. The birds are fitted with sharp spurs on their legs with which they attack the other bird until one is killed or unable to fight. There are three types of cockfight: the single battle in which two cocks fight; the main battle, where cocks are paired and play an elimination game; and the battle royal, in which several cocks fight each other until only one is standing. The Coliseo de Gallos in Lima hosts fights most weekends.

## SAPO

*Sapo* is a popular local game in Peru that is played in *picanterías* ("pee-kahn-tuh-REE-ahs"), or small local restaurants, and is as common as pool in the United States. *Sapo* means toad, and the game uses a large metal toad mounted on a table. Players throw brass discs as close to the toad as possible. The highest score is obtained when the disc is thrown into the toad's open mouth. Men can spend the whole afternoon, and evening, drinking beer and *chicha* and competing in this old game.

## *MOUNTAINEERING AND TREKKING*

The Andes was an impassable problem rather than a source of pleasure until the turn of the century, when climbing and hiking through the mountains became a popular pastime. More than 30 peaks rise well above 20,000 feet (6,090 meters) in a region that can only be compared to the Himalayas. The most beautiful views are found by climbing the Cordillera Blanca. Yet all mountaineering in this area is for the adventurous because of the obvious danger and the problems of high-altitude sickness.

Hikers along the Incan trail. Here trekkers can wander along paths that have been used for centuries, although they may have to make room for herds of goats or llamas.

# FESTIVALS

THE WORD *FIESTA* IS SPANISH for feast and is usually associated with the celebration of a religious event. Holidays are often accompanied by dancing, feasting, and music. Church bells ring, fireworks explode, processions begin and end, and eating and drinking never stop. Beneath all this gaiety, there is sometimes a serious reason for the festival.

Today, fiestas are held not only to commemorate a religious event but also to mark tribal or national occasions. The least entertaining are those connected with national holidays. The Day of National Honor on October 9 and the Independence Days on July 28–29 are the most important national holidays. They are occasions for speeches and military parades and a chance for local politicians to campaign.

Church festivals, on the other hand, are bright, colorful, energetic events, and far more popular. The Holy Week processions at Ayacucho attract people from all over the world.

The fiesta is an opportunity to bring color and laughter into lives that are often a hard struggle. Whether the celebration is wholly Christian, partly native, or a blend of African, Spanish, and Incan rituals, the fiesta is there to be enjoyed by everyone. A festival occurs only once a year, and because of this it is eagerly awaited by all. It is a project for all of the community to take part in and look forward to, when the poverty and hard work of everyday life are momentarily forgotten.

*Opposite:* **A woman in native dress at Inti Raymi.**

*Below:* **The Corpus Cristi festival in Cuzco.**

## COMMUNITY FIESTAS

Nearly every community has its own saint or patron figure, who often means a great deal more to local people than those connected to larger events. In the mountains and in small villages everywhere, the patron saint's day for that village is a splendid occasion and a well-earned holiday for the workers. The early Spanish missionaries, who were keen to get rid of the Incan religion, chose a saint's day that coincided with the most important pagan festival in each village, town, and city. This enabled them to change the pagan festival into an event of Christian significance.

**A village festival in the highlands. Festivals range from elaborate to very simple.**

### CALENDAR OF FESTIVALS

| | |
|---|---|
| January 1 | New Year's Day |
| January 6 | Epiphany |
| February | (First two weeks) Candlemas Festival |
| | The Fiesta de la Virgen de la Candelaria in Puno |
| February–March | Carnival |
| March–April | Easter, Maundy Thursday, Good Friday |
| May 1 | Labor Day |
| June | (Ninth Thursday after Easter) Corpus Cristi |
| June 24 | Inti Raymi in Cuzco |
| June 29 | Saints Peter and Paul |
| July 28–29 | Independence Days |
| August 15 | Feast of the Assumption |
| August 30 | Santa Rosa of Lima, patron saint of Peru |
| October 8 | Battle of Angamos |
| October 18 | Lord of the Miracles in Lima |
| November 1 | All Saints' Day |
| December 8 | Feast of the Immaculate Conception |
| December 25 | Christmas |

A special type of fiesta is known as the *feria* ("FAY-ree-ah"), which means fair or market in Spanish. The *feria* usually falls on a weekday when no festival occurs. There is a solemn reason for feast days, but the *feria* is mainly for entertainment, although masses are often said.

Religious festivals generally include a great fair or market, fireworks, bullfights, communal dancing with the peasants in traditional dress, roast pig, and lots of *chicha*. Special masses are often said, sometimes combined with a procession that includes carrying a saint's statue or other holy images. Market days frequently coincide with fiestas so as to allow local vendors to sell their wares to a large crowd.

Some of the most elaborate and colorful festivals are those belonging to the native peoples and the minority groups of blacks, Chinese, and Japanese who populate Peru. The September fiesta in Trujillo combines Andalusian, African, and native music with skillful dancing. These dances are performed in *peñas* all over the country, but rarely are they performed as well as they are in Trujillo.

Dancing at the September festival in Chincheros. Folk dancing, besides being a social entertainment, is a way of bringing the community together, both young and old, women and men.

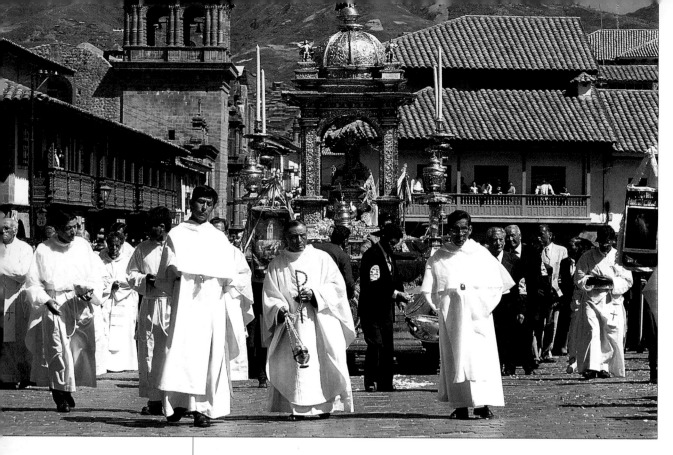

Priests leading the Corpus Cristi procession in Cuzco.

*June is the climax of the festival season in Cuzco, with two important Incan and Church festivals: Inti Raymi and Corpus Cristi.*

## FIESTAS IN CUZCO

Cuzco has an important fiesta occurring nearly every month. One of the oldest fiestas originated on March 31, 1650, when Cuzco was shattered by a major earthquake. A small statue known as *Nuestro Señor de los Temblores* ("NWAY-stro say-NYOR day los taym-BLOH-rays," Our Lord of the Earthquakes) was brought out and paraded around the city. The people believed this to have saved them from further destruction. Every year since then, on the first Monday of Holy Week, this statue of Christ, known to the natives as *Taitacha* ("tye-TAH-chah," Little Father), is carried on the three-hour circuit of Cuzco.

Corpus Cristi occurs on the Thursday after Trinity Sunday. The day before this, 13 statues of saints are brought from their respective churches in the suburbs or *barrios* ("BAH-ree-os") of Cuzco. They are borne on enormous litters followed by praying devotees and led by brass bands and parishioners who carry banners and candles. On Corpus Cristi, the Plaza de Armas is filled with the faithful, some of whom come hundreds of miles to be there. Large altars decorated with flowers, mirrors, crosses—and images of the sun, a remnant of Incan heritage—are erected on three sides of the plaza.

After high mass, the statues are paraded around the plaza on their litters until each has bowed to all the others. These litters can weigh up to a ton because of their gold and silver decorations. The litter is followed by other parishioners in brightly colored festival clothes and by musicians. Sometimes old women sing hymns in Quechua.

## CARNIVAL

*Carnavales* ("kar-nah-VAH-lays") is a great, joyous explosion celebrated throughout Peru. The word *carnival* comes from the Latin *carne vale,* which means "farewell to the flesh." Carnival is the last opportunity for people to drink, dance, and be merry before the fasting period of Lent.

The Quechua term for Carnavales is *jatum pujllay* ("ja-TUM POOJ-lay"), which translates as "the great game." This originates from the native tradition of rounding up wild game for presentation to the parish priest and the mayor, who in return provided *chicha* and coca leaves. Today, because game is less plentiful, lambs and farm animals are usually offered. The offering of the game is a fertility symbol going back to Incan days, when the Incas gave offerings and sacrifices to their gods in anticipation of a good harvest. The idea of fertility survives today, as Carnival is still regarded by many as the best opportunity for meeting or courting future husbands and wives.

**Corpus Cristi in Cuzco. The litters are carried by the parishioners of the church to which the statue belongs. It is regarded as a great honor to be a litter bearer.**

*Above*: **The Inca emperor is brought in for Inti Raymi.**

*Opposite*: **Musicians in traditional dress at Inti Raymi.**

## INTI RAYMI

Inti Raymi (Father Sun), on June 24, is the Incan celebration of the winter solstice, when the sun is farthest from the earth, and is dedicated to prayers for the return of the sun. The Incas believed that the sun regulated the universe and controlled the lives of plants, animals, and people. The modern native still believes that the sun and moon are gods capable of punishing or helping people.

Because the saint's day for St. John the Baptist falls on the 24th, the Spanish simply converted the ancient festival into a Christian one. Remnants of the original Incan festival still survive: fires left burning throughout the night of the 23rd are not in praise of St. John, but to bring back the sun after the longest night of the year.

The Inti Raymi of today was recreated in the 1940s based on descriptions of the early colonists, who had written down eyewitness reports. Before the ceremony, someone is chosen to be emperor of all the Incas and brought into Sacsayhuamán fortress on a litter. The emperor has a palace guard (composed of members of the Peruvian army in Incan costume) and traditionally dressed dancers who dance before him, recreating an ancient battle that ended in victory. The pageant begins, and a ceremony is made of relighting the fires, symbolic of the return of the emperor and the Incas. People also burn their old clothes as a symbol of an end to poverty, marking the year's harvest and the beginning of the new year. A llama is sacrificed to the sun (but not killed), and music and dancing go on for three hours. For the rest of the week, the city celebrates.

## DANCERS OF THE DEVIL IN PUNO

The department of Puno is in the densely populated but poor southernmost part of Peru bordering Lake Titicaca and Bolivia. It is the folk center of Peru and boasts a wide range of handicraft, legends, costumes, and dances. There are over 300 ethnic dances performed here, some of which are rarely seen by outsiders. The dances are usually reserved for the annual fiestas, especially Church festivals, although they date from preconquest days. Many of them originally concerned the agricultural life of the people and celebrated planting or harvest time.

Although most of the dances are complex, what is most apparent about the dancers is their elaborate costumes. These are extremely rich, embroidered, and ornate and are often the most expensive single item the family owns. As well as traditional indigenous costumes with their bowler hats and whirling skirts, dress also includes grotesque masks, sequined uniforms, and animal costumes—all in bright native colors.

The native peoples in this part of the world are accustomed to great hardship, and thus they celebrate their few holidays with great enthusiasm. During the feast of the Virgin of Candelaria or Candelmas, the Dance of the Devil can be seen. Expensive and horrible masks are worn by dancers who compete fiercely to outdance each other in the *Diablada* ("dee-ah-BLAH-dah"). The dancers gesticulate and contort their bodies into horrible positions and frighten the children. This dance probably dates to pre-Incan civilizations, its original meaning lost in time.

# FOOD

PERU'S VARIED CLIMATE AND GEOGRAPHY have produced the most extensive and varied menu in South America. Added to these geographic differences are differences in the diet of the rich and poor, the poor eating in the style of the ancient Incas, when corn, peppers, and potatoes were most important, the rich eating a blend of native and European cooking that evolved into the style of cuisine known as *criolla* ("cree-OH-lah").

Specializing in spicy food, modern Peru has many local delicacies from seafood on the coast to old Incan recipes such as roast guinea pig in peanut sauce. But the main foods, on which most of the population survive, are peppers, potatoes, and grains.

The ancient civilizations show in their pottery and weaving the primary cultural importance that food took in the community. Priests in pre-Incan societies decided the time for planting based on astral predictions.

*Ancient peoples would often bury food with their dead so as to sustain them on their journey to the next life. The Aymará around Lake Titicaca still stuff coca leaves in potatoes and bury them as a sacrifice to the earth mother,* Pacha Mama.

*Opposite*: **A *chicha* vendor in Urubamba. In ancient times, the Chosen Women, who were picked by priests to serve the Incan rulers, were the only people allowed to prepare this drink.**

*Left*: **The Sunday vegetable market in the main square of Pisac.**

115

*Even today, new varieties of potatoes are being discovered and exported. These new exports include the yellow* Limeña *potato, the* olluco, *which ranges in color from red, pink, and orange to white, and the potato with a purple skin that reveals an equally purple potato beneath.*

## POTATOES, CORN, AND PEPPERS

Because the coast is too arid to grow many crops and the Amazon jungle is too densely forested to be cultivated, the majority of the crops come from the highlands. Potatoes are indigenous to the Andes and were exported from the highland regions to Europe and the rest of the Americas beginning in the 16th century. There are over 200 varieties, some completely unknown outside the Andes. A farmer with a small holding may plant up to three dozen different varieties in one field.

Some potatoes grow at over 8,000 feet (2,500 meters), having adapted to that height and grown frost resistant. People in the highlands freeze-dry their potato crop to ensure that food is available later in the season. The potatoes are frozen on the ground in the evening when the temperature is below zero and then thawed out the next day as the sun warms the air; they are then frozen again that night. This process continues until they are completely dehydrated. The potato becomes dry and cardboard-like. It is then stored and can be kept for up to four years. These potatoes are popular in stews, where they are cooked like any other vegetable.

Different varieties of corn. Purple corn is traditionally used to make *chicha*. Another type of *chicha*, a thick white variety, is poured on the earth during harvest and planting rituals in the highlands.

Corn comes in as many varieties as the potato. It was regarded as sacred to the pre-Hispanic peoples. It was used for bartering and as a form of currency, as well as for eating.

Hot peppers are found in many varieties and lavishly used in everything from fish to soups. Marketplaces become a dazzling display of color as enormous baskets full of peppers in sun-yellow, flaming orange, fiery red, and green are sold and bought. On the coast, where fish is common in the diet, sauces of onions and peppers are offered in side bowls as condiments or heaped straight onto the meal. In the Amazon area, food is a little less spicy, but people still dip vegetables in pepper sauces. But it is in the highland area that the *picante* ("pee-KAHN-tay") or spicy form of cooking reaches an art form. Dishes are often laid out in degrees of spiciness according to the chili pepper used, ranging from the bland to the volcanic.

It is believed that South American natives originally grew five different types of pepper and these gradually made their way to Central America, Mexico, and the Caribbean. They were mistakenly called peppers by early Spanish explorers, who were looking for black pepper. They found the natives addicted to eating peppers at every meal and soon began to export them to Europe, Africa, and Asia. In India they became a staple in cooking.

*Grains such as the purple-flowered kiwacha and golden-brown quinoa disappeared for centuries under Spanish rule. The reason for this was that they were used in ceremonies, and when the Catholic Church banned the Incan religion, they also banned the grain. Besides taking away a part of their culture, the Spanish also took away a nourishing food source high in protein. Today, native peoples use these grains once again.*

## TRADITIONAL CUISINE

Local dishes are often called *criolla*, or Creole, meaning they are a mixture of Spanish and indigenous cuisines. *A la criolla* also refers to spicy foods. Many peoples have contributed to Peruvian cuisine: black slaves from the West Indies and Africa, Polynesian slaves from the Pacific Islands, Chinese and Japanese immigrants, and of course, Spanish and native peoples.

*Piqueo* ("pee-KAY-oh"), or appetizers, are a speciality of Peru and are frequently so large that there is little room for the main course. A favorite *piqueo* is Arequipa-style potatoes, or *Papas Arequipeña*. These are potatoes boiled, sliced, and served with a peanut, cheese, and chili sauce.

**A set lunch includes chicken soup, meat, rice, and a drink.**

Most entrées are dips, and you can mix them and have many varieties at one sitting.

There are also unusual Peruvian dishes. *Anticuchos* ("an-tee-KOO-chohs") are skewers of ox heart with hot peppers and seasoning barbecued over glowing coals. This dish is usually available from street vendors. Another unusual speciality is *Causa a la Limeña* ("COW-sah ah lah lee-MAY-nyah"), made from yellow potatoes, cornmeal, pork, olives, onions, boiled eggs, peppers, sweet potatoes, prawns, and cheese.

Smoked fish is popular, especially smoked trout from the highlands. In the Pachamanca style of cooking, a truly Peruvian cuisine, meat and frequently fish are cooked by wrapping them in leaves, usually banana, and steaming them beneath layers of earth and coal.

One of the best desserts is *Mazamorra Marada* ("mah-zah-MOH-rah mah-RAH-dah"), which is a sweet casserole made from pineapples, peaches, apples, dried fruit, quinces, sugar, and purple corn. It is served hot and sprinkled with lemon juice and cinnamon.

Preparing food in Ollantaytambo, in Cuzco. Typical highland dishes include *cuy* ("KWEE," guinea pig), which is usually roasted, as well as delicious corn tamales with cow's brains. In the central highlands *Papa a la Huancaína* is very popular, consisting of boiled potatoes with a white sauce of cheese, milk, hot peppers, and butter. This is served with olives and eaten like a potato salad.

## REGIONAL DELICACIES

Authentic Peruvian cuisine is more likely to be served in the highlands, especially in Cuzco. Dishes include *rocoto relleno* ("roh-COH-toh ray-YAY-noh," spicy bell peppers stuffed with ground beef and vegetables), *chicharrones* ("chee-chah-ROH-nays," deep-fried chunks of pork rib called *chauco* or chicken called *gallina*), *choclo con queso* ("CHOH-cloh kon KAY-so," corn on the cob with cheese), and the obligatory *tamales*.

In the Amazon basin, people eat *farina,* a muesli-like yucca eaten fried or mixed with lemonade. In the markets, children sell hot *pan de arroz* ("pahn day ah-ROHZ"), a bread made from rice flour, yucca, and butter that takes three days to prepare. Some specialities of the region include *juanes* ("HWAH-nays," fish or chicken steamed in a banana leaf with rice or yucca) and *chocann* ("CHOH-can," a soup of fish chunks flavored with cilantro). Fish dishes are popular, and the Amazon provides everything from the small flesh-eating piranhas to the huge *paiches* ("PIE-chays").

On the coast and in the desert region, food is prepared in the same hearty manner as in the highlands, but with fish, chicken, or goat instead of beef. A favorite dish is roast kid cooked with *chicha* and served with beans and rice. But the best coastal dishes are those containing seafood. *Ceviche*, or marinated whitefish, is the most traditional.

*Fish is believed to have rejuvenating power, and a thick rice and fish soup (aguadito) is traditionally served to all-night party-goers. Signs on street stalls often promise "Aguadito to recuperate energy."*

**A quick meal is served in the Cuzco food market.**

---

*In the Andes, cooking is more difficult. Air has less pressure at high altitudes, and recipes have to be changed. The change in altitude mostly affects foods that require baking or boiling or that contain a lot of sugar.*

## DINING OUT

In most villages local restaurants called *picanterías* (literally "spicy places" because of the use of peppers) or *quintas* ("KEEN-tahs," country houses) serve typical dishes of the area. Most of the *picanterías* are open only two or three days a week, but because there are so many, one at least is always open. Live music is often played, and they are usually the social center of many communities. *Quintas* provide the same service in the suburbs. Another popular type of restaurant and one that shows Peru's ethnic diversity is the *chifas* ("CHEE-fahs"), or Chinese restaurants, that dot the coastal towns, making noodles part of the staple diet in some parts of Peru. Of a more basic nature are taverns called *chicherías* ("chee-cha-REE-ahs"), named after the Andean speciality *chicha*, the corn beer. They also serve meals and snacks.

Peruvian streets are often filled with street vendors selling shish kebabs, fish—in fact, anything that's portable and edible. Generally, Peruvians have a very sweet tooth and indulge themselves in the many desserts sold on the streets, like *churro* ("CHOO-roh," a deep-fried tube of pastry filled with honey), *revolución caliente* ("ray-voh-loo-SYON kah-lee-AIN-tay," crunchy, spicy cookies), or in the summer, cones of crushed ice flavored with fruit syrups, which are available on every street corner.

## DRINKS

Tap water in South America is not completely safe. Although it may come from a chlorination or filtration plant, the pipes that bring it to the tap are usually old, cracked, or contain dirt. Most people drink bottled water, although it is frequently the carbonated kind.

## CEVICHE

This dish has been eaten on the Peruvian coast for at least the last thousand years. Marinating raw fish in lime juice has the same effect as cooking, but be sure to marinate it long enough or it could be dangerous to eat. The fish becomes white and firm, with the appearance of cooked fish. This dish is usually served as an entrée or for lunch.

2 pounds (900 grams) of white fish fillet (sea bass preferably), cut into small pieces

juice of six limes
2 large onions, sliced thinly
1 tablespoon olive oil
1 tablespoon fresh cilantro
1 clove garlic, crushed
1–2 chilies, chopped finely
black pepper
1 teaspoon salt

Mix the lime juice with the onion slices, oil, cilantro, garlic, chilies, pepper, and salt in a bowl.

Place the fish in a shallow glass or ceramic dish and pour the spice mixture over it. The fish must be covered; if not, more juice should be added.

Cover tightly and refrigerate for several hours (or overnight) until the fish is "soft cooked."

Serve on lettuce leaves garnished with onion rings, thin strips of red pepper, and sweet potatoes and/or corn on the cob.

Tea is usually served black with lemon and sugar. Peru grows its own coffee, but it does not generally have the excellence of that grown in neighboring Colombia. The favorite method of making coffee is to boil it for hours until only a thick dark syrup remains, called *essencia*. This is poured into cruets and diluted with hot milk or water.

Besides many of the usual varieties of soft drinks (or *gaseosas*, "gah-say-OH-sas") sold in the United States, Peru also has its own varieties, which are very sweet. Local favorites are Inca Cola, a gold-colored soda, and Cola Inglesa, which is red and very sweet. Fruit juices are very common and come in many exotic flavors: blackberry, passionfruit, and watermelon, to name a few.

Most people, especially in rural areas, drink *chicha*. This beer is made by fermenting corn or quinoa. Some of the recipes date back to the Incas. A red or white bunch of flowers or a plastic bag on a pole outside a house indicates that *chicha* is for sale there.

*Hot chocolate is excellent in Peru, where cocoa beans are grown.*

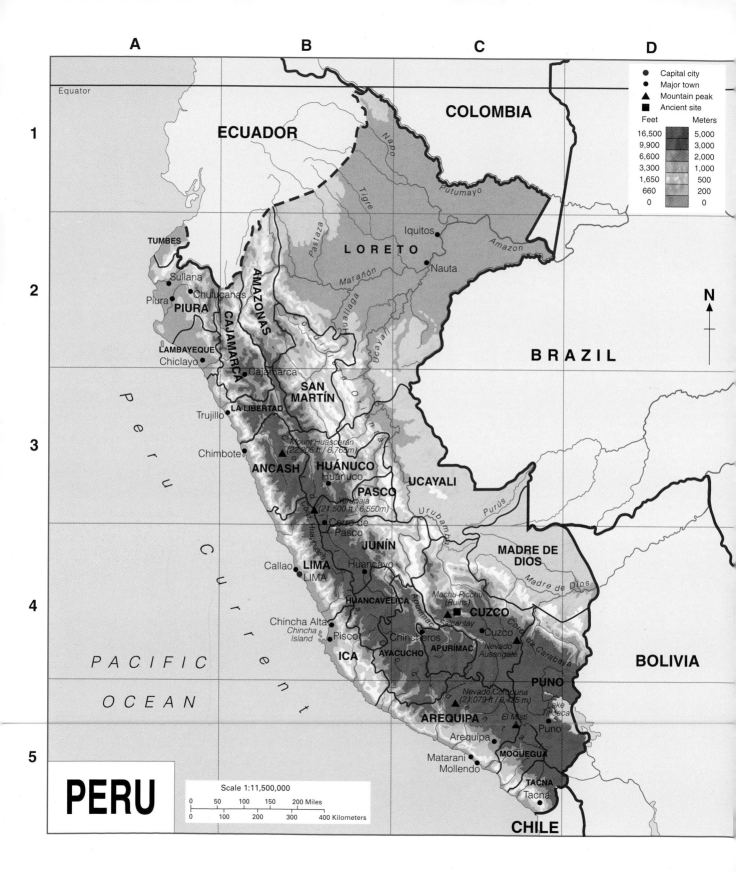

A     B     C     D

Equator

**ECUADOR**

**COLOMBIA**

1

Napo

| | Capital city |
| | Major town |
| ▲ | Mountain peak |
| ■ | Ancient site |

Feet     Meters
16,500    5,000
9,900    3,000
6,600    2,000
3,300    1,000
1,650    500
660    200
0    0

Tigre

Putumayo

TUMBES

Iquitos

**L O R E T O**

Amazon

Sullana

Pastaza

Nauta

Marañon

2

Piura • Chulucanas

**PIURA**

**AMAZONAS**

Huallaga

Ucayali

**B R A Z I L**

N

**CAJAMARCA**

**LAMBAYEQUE**

Chiclayo •

Cajamarca •

**SAN
MARTÍN**

Trujillo •
**LA LIBERTAD**

Mount Huascarán
(22,205 ft / 6,768m)

3

Chimbote •

**ANCASH**

**HUÁNUCO**

Huánuco •

**UCAYALI**

**PASCO**

Yerupajá
(21,500 ft / 6,550m)

Urubamba

Purús

Cerro de
Pasco •

**JUNÍN**

Callao •

**LIMA**

Huancayo •

**MADRE DE
DIOS**

Madre de Dios

LIMA

4

**HUANCAVELICA**

Machu Picchu
(Ruins)

Apurímac

■ **CUZCO**

Chincha Alta •
Chincha
Island

Pisco •

Chincheros •

**AYACUCHO**

**APURÍMAC**

Salcantay ▲

Cuzco •

Nevado
Ausangate ▲

Cordillera de Carabaya

**BOLIVIA**

**ICA**

**PUNO**

**P A C I F I C**

Nevado Coropuna
(21,079 ft / 6,425m) ▲

Lake
Titicaca

**O C E A N**

**AREQUIPA**

El Misti ▲

Puno •

Arequipa •

5

Matarani •
Mollendo •

**MOQUEGUA**

**PERU**

Scale 1:11,500,000

0   50   100   150   200 Miles

0   100   200   300   400 Kilometers

**TACNA**

Tacna •

**CHILE**

Peru Current

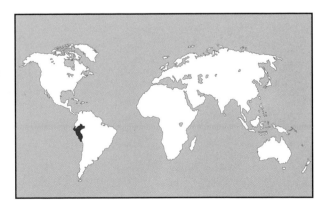

# QUICK NOTES

**OFFICIAL NAME**
República del Perú (Republic of Peru)

**LAND AREA**
496,222 square miles
(1,285,215 square kilometers)

**POPULATION**
23 million

**CAPITAL**
Lima

**DEPARTMENTS**
Amazonas, Ancash, Apurímac, Arequipa, Ayacucho, Cajamarca, Callao, Cuzco, Huancavelica, Huánuco, Ica, Junín, La Libertad, Lambayeque, Lima, Loreto, Madre de Dios, Moquegua, Pasco, Piura, Puno, San Martín, Tacna, Tumbes, Ucayali

**IMPORTANT CITIES**
Lima, Arequipa, Callao, Trujillo, Chiclayo, Piura, Chimbote

**MAJOR RIVERS**
Ucayali, Marañón, Amazon

**MAJOR LAKE**
Lake Titicaca

**MAJOR GEOGRAPHIC REGIONS**
Costa (coastal region)
Sierra (Andes region)
Selva (rainforest region)

**HIGHEST POINT**
Mt. Huascarán (22,205 ft/6,765 m)

**MAJOR RELIGION**
Roman Catholicism

**OFFICIAL LANGUAGES**
Spanish and Quechua

**MAIN EXPORTS**
Copper, fishmeal, zinc, oil, lead, coffee

**CURRENCY**
Nuevo sol
$1 = 2.19 nuevos soles

**IMPORTANT ANNIVERSARIES**
Labor Day (May 1)
Independence Days (July 28–29)
St. Rose of Lima (August 30)

**POLITICAL LEADERS**
Francisco Pizarro (c. 1478–1541), Spanish conqueror of the Incas
José de San Martín (1778–1850), Liberator of Peru
Simon Bolívar (1783–1830), First president
Javier Pérez de Cuéllar, former Secretary General of the United Nations
Alberto Fujimori (1946–), Current president

**LEADERS IN THE ARTS**
César Vallejo (1892–1938), poet
Mario Vargas Llosa (1936–), novelist, playwright, critic
Roca Rey (1923–), sculptor
Fernando de Szyszlo (1925–), painter

# GLOSSARY

**barrio** ("BAH-ree-oh")
District, neighborhood, or suburb.

**chicha** ("CHEE-chah")
Beer made from fermented corn.

**cholo** ("CHOH-loh")
Indigenous person trying to join mestizo society.

**coca** ("COH-cah")
Plant from which cocaine is made. The leaves are often chewed by Andean people to relieve hunger, cold, or fatigue.

**compadres** ("kom-PAH-drays")
Godparents.

**Creole**
Person of Spanish descent born in the Americas.

**encomenderos** ("en-koh-men-DER-ohs")
Local village chiefs in colonial times.

**encomienda** ("en-koh-MYEN-dah")
System instituted by the Spanish colonizers: land was given to a Spaniard, who had the right to force the natives living there to work.

**feria** ("FAY-ree-ah")
Fair or market in the Sierra.

**hacienda**
Ranch or farming estate.

**hispanistas** ("ees-pan-EES-tahs")
Artists using a Spanish-derived style.

**huaquero** ("wah-KAY-roh")
Person who robs precolonial temples, burial sites, or shrines.

**indigenistas** ("een-dee-hain-EES-tahs")
Artists using native subjects for their work.

**machismo** ("mah-CHEES-moh")
Belief in male strength and superiority.

**manta** ("MAHN-tah")
Shoulder wrap worn by Andean women.

**mate** ("MAH-tay")
An herbal tea.

**mestizo** ("mes-TEE-zoh")
Person of mixed Spanish and native origin.

**núcleos** ("NOO-kle-ohs")
Education center in remote areas.

**picante** ("pee-KAHN-tay")
Spicy; a style of cooking spicy foods.

**peña** ("PAY-nyah")
Music hall or nightclub.

**quipu** ("KEE-poo")
System of knotted string that Incas used for communication.

**reducciones** ("ray-duc-SYO-nays")
Artificial towns created by Spanish colonizers for native peoples.

**Selva**
Amazon region east of the Andes.

**Sendero Luminoso**
("sen-DER-oh loo-mee-NOH-soh")
"Shining Path," a guerrilla group.

**shaman**
Village healer providing herbal medicine.

**Sierra**
Mountainous Andes region running through the center of Peru.

# BIBLIOGRAPHY

Fisher, John R., ed. *Peru*. Santa Barbara, California: ABC-CLIO, 1990.

Hudson, Rex A. *Peru, A Country Study*. Washington, D.C.: U.S. Government Printing Office, 1993.

Lepthein, Emilie U. *Peru*. Chicago: Children's Press, 1992.

Lerner Publications Co. *Peru in Pictures*. Minneapolis, MN: Lerner Publications Co., 1992.

Meyerson, Julia. *Tambo: Life in an Andean Village*. Austin: University of Texas Press, 1990.

Norman, Ruth and Charles Spaegel. *The Last Inca—Atahualpa: An Eye-Witness Account of the Conquest of Peru*. El Cajon, California: Unarius Publications, 1993.

# INDEX

# INDEX

# INDEX

## PICTURE CREDITS